"I have a dream that my four children will one day live in a nation where they will not be judged by the color of their skin, but by the content of their character."

Martin Luther King

I have a dream

words to change the world

- MOTIVATE your pupils to write and appreciate poetry.
- INSPIRE them to share their hopes and dreams for the future.
- BOOST awareness of your school's creative ability.
- WORK alongside the National Curriculum or the high level National Qualification Skills.
- Supports the *Every Child Matters - Make a Positive Contribution* outcome.
- Over £7,000 of great prizes for schools and pupils.

"When I was out there I was never ever alone, there was always a team of people behind me, in mind if not in body."

Ellen MacArthur

Dorset
Edited by Heather Killingray

 Young**Writers**

First published in Great Britain in 2006 by:
Young Writers
Remus House
Coltsfoot Drive
Peterborough
PE2 9JX
Telephone: 01733 890066
Website: www.youngwriters.co.uk

SB ISBN 1 84602 493 5

Foreword

Imagine a teenager's brain; a fertile yet fragile expanse teeming with ideas, aspirations, questions and emotions. Imagine a classroom full of racing minds, scratching pens writing an endless stream of ideas and thoughts . . .

. . . Imagine your words in print reaching a wider audience. Imagine that maybe, just maybe, your words can make a difference. Strike a chord. Touch a life. Change the world. Imagine no more . . .

'I Have a Dream' is a series of poetry collections written by 11 to 18-year-olds from schools and colleges across the UK and overseas. Pupils were invited to send us their poems using the theme 'I Have a Dream'. Selected entries range from dreams they've experienced to childhood fantasies of stardom and wealth, through inspirational poems of their dreams for a better future and of people who have influenced and inspired their lives.

The series is a snapshot of who and what inspires, influences and enthuses young adults of today. It shows an insight into their hopes, dreams and aspirations of the future and displays how their dreams are an escape from the pressures of today's modern life. Young Writers are proud to present this anthology, which is truly inspired and sure to be an inspiration to all who read it.

Contents

Beaucroft Foundation School

Emma Farrell (12)	1
Sophie Houghton (11)	1
Zoë Hunt (13)	1
Scott Willis (12)	2
Amy Pickford (12)	2
Diana Cutting (13)	3
Kelly O'Hara (13)	3

Broadstone Middle School

Matthew Brunnock (12)	4
Brianna Bartlett (11)	4
Isobel Tiffin (11)	5
Rehana Begum (11)	5
Kathryn Pritchard (10)	6
Alexandra Herron (10)	6
Stephanie Woolgar (11)	7
Claire Harling (11)	8
Anya Blanshard (12)	9
Ryan Cooper (11)	10
Ross Newitt (13)	10
Ellie Sheppard (11)	11
Maxwell Vincent (13)	11
Max Rycroft (12)	12
Hannah Cooksley (12)	13
Alex Bonner (11)	14
Emma Lewns (11)	15
Zoë Mattacks (12)	16
Ben Moyse (12)	17
Jez Atkin (11)	17
Jessica Girvin (11)	18
Alex Fair (12)	19
Alex Huntley (12)	19
Matt Copp (13)	20
Mark Sandford (11)	21
Benjamin Judge (12)	21
Gary Brushett (13)	22
Alexandra Hughes (12)	23
Oscar Borton (11)	24

Samantha Bumford (13)   24
Jack Durham (11)   25
Bethanie Gomm (12)   25
Conner Ross-Read (12)   26
Ashley Jacobs (12)   26
Cassie Marshall (13)   27
Jonathan Arnekleiv (12)   27
Eloise Towning (11)   28
Alex Cox (11)   29
Drew Giggins (11)   29
Emily Worssell (12)   30
Nick Phelps (12)   31
Joe Shackleton (13)   32
Ben Evans (13)   32
Jonathan Sparks (12)   33
Bradley Ripley (10)   33
Grace Tyror (13)   34
Ryan Quick (12)   35
John Fessey (12)   36
Thomas Pearce (12)   36
Adam Denison (13)   37
Ruby Bissagar (11)   37
Elizabeth Smart (13)   38
Fiona Bustard (12)   39
Charlotte Durant (11)   40
Suzanna French (12)   41
Meg Selby (12)   42
Brittany French (11)   43
Adam Stroud (11)   44
Deborah Smith (13)   45
Kate Hennessy (13)   46
Kathryn Pritchard (10)   46
Rachael Paton (12)   47
Dominic Wood (11)   47
Natasha Underwood (12)   48
James Carter (11)   48
Emily King-Underwood (13)   49
Megan King (11)   49
Rio-Taya Courtenay-Lewis (11)   50
Ben Hutton (12)   50
Jack Clements (11)   51
Lauren Ayers (12)   51

Hannah Newey (11)	52
Carys Digby (11)	52
Joseph Cross (12)	53
Tom Brophy (12)	53
Josh Perren (12)	54
Hayley Cornish (13)	55
Abigail Wassell (11)	55
Emily Parsons (12)	56
Ellie Hilborne (11)	57
Connor Hallisey (11)	58
Oliver Smith (11)	59
Lauren Trent (10)	60
Stevie Addicott (13)	61
Eleanor Pilborough (11)	62
Becky Troke (12)	62
Rebecca Matcham (12)	63
Elliot Talbot (11)	63
Sam Essam (11)	64
Anya Levkouskis (13)	65
Gregory Perkins (12)	66
Charlotte Roberts (12)	67
Emily Phillips (11)	68
Chantelle Evans (11)	69

Bryanston School

Laura Tenwick (14)	69
Alice Whitlock (14)	70
Becca Scott (14)	71

Cranborne Middle School

Anna Moses (13)	72
Kelie Petterssen (13)	73
Hannah Deacon (13)	74
Mat Williets (13)	75
Samantha Roberts (13)	76
Rebecca Withers (13)	77
Amy Lawrence (13)	78
Katie Davies (12)	78
Fiona Penny (12)	79
Holly Morgan (13)	80
Georgina Towler (13)	80

Mike Wale (13)   81
Rosie Campbell (13)   82
Joel Williams (12)   83
Lucy Sparrow (12)   84

Lytchett Minster School
Thomas Rodwell (11)   84
Chelsea Venier (12)   85
Liam Murray (13)   85
Georgia Marshall (11)   86
Lucy Benjafield (11)   86
William Gilligan (14)   87
Ross Chirnside (13)   87
Liam Mullany (13)   88
Alex Lovell (14)   89
Helen Ellis (14)   90

Sherborne School for Girls
Antonia Hollis (14)   91
Helena Maitland-Robinson (13)   92
Louise Crowley (14)   92
Pippa Jenkins (13)   93
Alice Hayes (13)   93
Tatiana Elwes (14)   94
Emma Welsh (14)   94
Georgia Horrocks (14)   95
Emily Rainbow (13)   96
Alice Maltby (14)   97
Zoe Lodge (13)   97
Georgina Bolton Carter (13)   98

The Grange School
Jade Rickman (15)   98
Oliver Frampton (15)   99
Nick Gallop (15)   99
Chelsie Andrews (16)   100
Adam Burtenshaw (14)   100
Rosy Conner (15)   101
Daniel Sparkes (14)   101
Jonathan Bakes (15)   102

Rebecca Seymour (14)   102
Adam Dean (14)   103

Uplands School
Andrew Grantham (15)   103
Nabil Mahmoud (15)   104
Alexandra Guerra Unwin (16)   105
Chloe Everett (15)   105
Rhiannon Wilson (16)   106
Phoebe Bowman (15)   106
David Evans (14)   107
Chris Birtles (14)   107
Laura Edwards (15)   108
Daniel Bath (13)   108
Oliver Shrimpton (14)   109
Oliver Ricketts (11)   109
Ellen Walsh (16)   110
Christopher Tiernan (12)   110
Peter Dixon (16)   111
Otis Ooi (12)   111
Toby Adams (13)   112
William Evans (12)   112
Tim Johnson (13)   113
Jennie Bird (16)   113
Charlie Power (15)   114
Matthew Nisbet (14)   114
Brandon Andrews-Hewitt (13)   115
Piers Bate (16)   115
Toby Hoare (15)   116
Helen Day (15)   116
Toby Khalife (14)   117
Jessica Bishop (11)   117
Rachmat Akbar Triyadi (12)   118
Sophia Bird (11)   119
Jack Fuller (12)   120
Thomas Beesley (11)   121
Joshua Boer (10)   122
Isabel Breslin (11)   122
Megan Creed (10)   123
Georgie Rowbrey (11)   123
Megan Hallowes (10)   124

Jacob Webster (10)	125
Jack Notley (11)	126
Jonny Summerell (12)	126
Zack Dalton-Biggs (11)	127
Angharad Burn (11)	128
Jordana Coulstock (11)	129
Robert Bell (11)	129
Jack Kane (15)	130
Lewis Tottle (13)	130
Anthony Skilton (14)	131
Sam Hardinges (11)	131
James Creevy (14)	132
James Cull (10)	132

Wareham Middle School

Oliver McMillan (11)	133
Bethany Ritchie (12)	133
Rachel Woolley (11)	134
Holly Elliott (11)	135
Hattie Stewart (12)	136
Joseph Ely (11)	136
Molly Irwin (12)	137
Ella Ward (12)	137
Carly Hutchins (12)	138
Sam Duffield (11)	138
Alex Rainbird (11)	139
Martin Buxton (11)	139
Eden Midgley (11)	140
Charles Fishlock (12)	140
Daizee-Laine Napier (11)	141
Marcia Gaskell (12)	142
Cameron Slacke (12)	143

The Poems

I Had A Vision About A War

I had a vision about a war
That ends today
So no one gets hurt anymore
Hospitals have more beds for people
And the bombs stop destroying things
So help stop the war
Please, help my vision come true
Thank you.

Emma Farrell (12)
Beaucroft Foundation School

Wars

I would like to live in a world where
No people get hurt
I want people to stay at home
There is no fighting
Everybody has a happy day
I would like to live in a world where
Everyone has fun.

Sophie Houghton (11)
Beaucroft Foundation School

In The World

I would like to live in a world where
Wild animals are protected
Elephants are not killed for their tusks
Bird flu is not a problem
People are not killed in wars
I would like to live in a world where
It is peaceful and quiet.

Zoë Hunt (13)
Beaucroft Foundation School

In My World

In my world
Everyone will get on with each other
Everyone will use nice words
If we were all the same it would be boring.

In my world
No one will be at war
No one will get into fights
There will be no gangs and no one will try to kill anyone
And no one will swear.

In my world
Every animal will be kept alive
Every animal will be treated fairly.

In my world
Everything will be free.

Scott Willis (12)
Beaucroft Foundation School

I Wish . . .

I wish that people do not have disabilities.
I wish that the poor people had homes.
I wish that there were more wheelchairs and more guide dogs.
I wish there weren't be any wars.
I wish there were more kind people.
I wish the world could be a better place.

Amy Pickford (12)
Beaucroft Foundation School

Crime

There will be no more fighting
No more killing
Police will understand why people fight
And do their best to help.

There will be no more stealing
No more robberies
Everyone will be safe in their homes
And will never have to worry.

I have a dream
There will be no more crime.

Diana Cutting (13)
Beaucroft Foundation School

No Crime

N ations stop fighting
O ffer people education

C ars stop speeding
R obbery reduced
I nterview people's lives
M urders to stop
E verybody to have fun.

Kelly O'Hara (13)
Beaucroft Foundation School

I Have A Dream

I have a dream that there is peace on Earth,
A time to realise what people are worth.
No wars, no guns, bombs or blitz,
Where peace and security really exists.

I have a dream that people will care,
And when there's need, somebody's there.
With cures to all terrible diseases,
No cancer, cholera, bad colds and sneezes.

I have a dream that drugs aren't misused,
Where science and medicines gifts aren't abused.
Where people can get all the help that they need,
And the wealth of the world isn't controlled by greed.

I have a dream there would be no homeless;
To sleep in a shelter is a bonus.
There are family dinners and no empty seats;
This is my dream world, as my heart beats.

Matthew Brunnock (12)
Broadstone Middle School

Imagine

Imagine,
A world with fun, everyone enjoying the sun.

Imagine,
A world without murders, a world with kindness and forgiveness.

Imagine,
A world with no fighting or racism, just sharing.

Imagine,
A world with happiness and full of children's laughter.

Imagine,
A world with no homeless or starving.

Imagine if this was our world.
Which would you prefer; a million smiles or just a million faces?

Brianna Bartlett (11)
Broadstone Middle School

In My Utopia

There would be no smoky clouds
Floating around our heads;

Less dreary rain to bring our spirits down,
This would be the key to a happier me;

No noisy traffic to hear or smell,
Or fumes from cars,
Like a thick, greasy gel;

A snowflake will flutter, fall like a tear,
Landing too quietly for you to hear.

Racism and terrorism I predict,
Man and woman should not inflict.

Let's try to change the world forever
And try to make our lives much better.

Today I will save the world,
Tomorrow I will save the universe.

Isobel Tiffin (11)
Broadstone Middle School

I Dream

I dream of . . .

Peace for the world,
The world to be peace.

No mystery murders,
No more murders to be.

No debts, no dirt,
For everything to be free.

No poverty in the world,
For poverty to be peace.

That's what I dream,
I dream to be free.

Rehana Begum (11)
Broadstone Middle School

Which?

Think;
A million dollars or a million voices,
Which will change the world?

Hear;
A good listener or a constant talker,
Which will change the world?

See;
A kind giver or a harsh taker,
Which will change the world?

Taste;
Unfair or fair-trade products,
Which will change the world?

Touch;
A helping hand or a hurting word,
Which will change the world?

Smell;
A factory's fumes or nature's nourishment,
Which will change the world?

Which will change the world?

Kathryn Pritchard (10)
Broadstone Middle School

A Perfect World

A perfect world would look like a crystal ball of care and love.
A perfect world would feel as soft as a kitten, as white as a dove.
A perfect world would smell like a pure rose, as red as blood.
A perfect world would sound like a chaffinch leaving a flood.
A perfect world would taste as sweet as a ripe peach.
A perfect world would be as beautiful as a sun setting over the beach.

Alexandra Herron (10)
Broadstone Middle School

Imagine

We need to take care of our world today,
We can all help in our own little way.

No more pollution;
There is a solution;
Cleaner lives.

No more wars;
We have laws;
Happier lives.

No more smoking;
We're all choking;
Healthier lives.

Is this what you imagine too?
Which do you think is best for you?

Constant pollution;
Endangered lives.

Constant wars;
Dangerous lives.

Constant smoking;
Shortened lives.

What would be your choice?
We all have a voice.

Stephanie Woolgar (11)
Broadstone Middle School

I Have A Dream

I have a dream,
Why is poverty in this world?
Why won't it go away?
Imagine if it wasn't there!
I wish poor people in poverty would have a fair say!

Votes, homes and schools,
Votes on their country leaders,
Homes, even shelters would do
And schools somewhere for children to learn.
I wish poor people in poverty would have a fair say!

Why must the poor people in poverty get diseases?
AIDS could kill a mother, her children could die.
Why is it them?

What has this world turned into?
I can smell the fumes of the rich!
I can hear the children's cries,
But worst of all, I can see what's going on!
What has this world turned into?

We *can* do something!
Rich can give more to the poor,
Don't give to football and other sports,
This is more important.
We *can* do something!

I have a dream!
Why is poverty in this world?
Why won't it go away?
Imagine if it wasn't there!

Claire Harling (11)
Broadstone Middle School

I Had A Dream

I had a dream one night,
A dream that could come true,
That all the people in the dark,
Would be safe from trouble.

All the people out there,
Be true to yourself and friends,
Don't be racist and don't be unkind,
Otherwise you'll never mend.

Everyone has a nightmare,
A nightmare of death and sorrow,
But everyone has a fantasy,
Of what they want to do.

Is there a real need for wars?
If only they were just unreal!
Why don't our fantasies come true?
Or is there a real need?

Why do people complain
About our looks and weight?
Don't they realise the hurt they give
To others who want to be friends?

I had a dream one night,
A dream that could come true,
That all the people in the dark,
Would be safe from trouble and gloom.

Anya Blanshard (12)
Broadstone Middle School

I Had A Dream

I had a dream, it was about pollution
White trees in Kenya, all white and snowy
Icicles in Mexico, freezing temperatures
I don't see any care about the future

We could all just live underwater
But then where's the treacle syrup
We would all think

Boiling hot in Iceland and Antarctica
All ice melted
All of us underwater

The London taxis don't mind all the damage they are doing
As well as the lorry drivers
Just thinking about the money for their jobs

The all day use of cars we all use
We've got to admit only the sensible people don't have a licence
We have got to do something now or never.

Ryan Cooper (11)
Broadstone Middle School

I Had A Vision

I had a vision of the future,
Black and white people stood together,
No more racism was in the world.

I had a vision of the future,
The world was at peace,
There was no more war for everyone.

I had a vision of the future,
The world I saw in front of me was a united world,
All joined together to help make the world a better place.

I had a vision of the future,
The birds were singing loudly and the sun was shining brightly,
The clouds had finally gone away and left the world in peace.

Ross Newitt (13)
Broadstone Middle School

Young Writers - I Have A Dream Dorset

My Perfect World

My perfect world is in peace and harmony,
Where love is everywhere, all around;
Where there is no me and I, just us together.

My perfect world is where everyone is cherished,
Where no one is sad, frightened or forgotten;
Where hatred and greed aren't in the dictionary.

My perfect world is with friends and family,
Where racism doesn't exist;
Where anger never shows and nobody shouts.

My perfect world is where weapons are unheard of,
Where war hasn't been founded;
Where no one loses or wins.

My perfect world is where everyone is treated equally,
Where no fights take place;
Where everyone is beaming.

My perfect world is all of these things!

Ellie Sheppard (11)
Broadstone Middle School

I Had A Dream

In my dream world there would be groups of people,
There would be no violence, hunger or wars,
Everyone would be friendly, happy and cheerful,
It would be perfect.

In my dream world there would be a bubble around the world
To protect it from bad things.
It would be a world where nothing went bad at all,
It would be perfect.

In my dream world there would be clean water for everyone,
There would be a home for everyone, a roof over their head,
No more nights in the rain, it would be good if it were all true,
But it's just a dream.

Maxwell Vincent (13)
Broadstone Middle School

I Had A Dream

I had a dream
Of rolling hills
And fields of grass
All of it spoilt by steam and smoke
I lay on the ground to cough and choke.

I had a dream
Of no more illness
Millions saved from cancer
Hospitals are empty
And people live.

I had a dream
Of true democracy
Where we choose together
With no more housing parties
And no picky politicians.

I had a dream
With manners and respect
Honoured by decency and fairness
No more hoodlums or racism
A world where everyone is equal.

Max Rycroft (12)
Broadstone Middle School

I Dream

I dream of a world
With no wars or fighting
And that everyone can live
In harmony and peace
I dream of a world like this.

I dream of a world
With no shouting or crying
And for no one to feel left out of a group
I dream of a world like this.

I dream of a world
With no words that hurt
And that no one will fight and linger in violence
In hatred
I dream of a world like this.

I dream of this world
But when will it happen?
I will dream and I will dream
And no one can stop me
Until my point gets through.

Hannah Cooksley (12)
Broadstone Middle School

I Dreamt

I dreamt about green fields,
With no litter and no pollution,
And on that field I saw the sun rising,
The start of a new era for mankind.

I dreamt I saw the sea,
I saw all our sins washing away,
I do hope mankind can start again,
With no wars and no global arguments.

I dreamt about green fields,
With no litter and no pollution,
And on that field I saw the sun rising,
The start of a new era for mankind.

I dreamt about a volcano,
Letting out all our frustration and anger,
But I do hope it is not on other people,
Because if we did, we would destroy our world.

I dreamt about green fields,
With no litter and no pollution,
And on that field I saw the sun rising,
I do pray, this is a new era for mankind.

Alex Bonner (11)
Broadstone Middle School

I Had A Dream

Once I had a dream,
A very scary dream,
No wars, no wars,
I shouted in my head.

The bang of a gun,
Was like a sudden crack of a tree,
I wish it was safe,
I wish it was calm.

Once I had a dream,
A very scary dream,
No wars, no wars,
I shouted in my head.

A perfect world would be,
Like a sudden miracle,
No wars,
Just peace.

Once I had a dream,
A very scary dream,
No wars, no wars,
I shouted in my head.

This is my dream,
A very important one.

Emma Lewns (11)
Broadstone Middle School

I Dream

I dream of a world where everyone is free and equal,
Everyone is respected, no matter what,
All races, religions and acts wouldn't stand in the way,
Of anything,
It would be a wonderful world.

I dream of a world where no one is too poor or too rich,
No people living in poverty,
No people living too elaborate a life,
While others live with nothing of their own,
It would be a wonderful world.

I dream of a world where there are no wars happening,
No man-made disasters, killing people,
For no important reason,
Wars shouldn't be fought over a piece of land,
It would be a wonderful world.

I dream of a world where everyone is kind and helpful,
There is no point in being cruel to others,
As rain will fall in the driest desert,
To help a single flower grow.
It would be a wonderful world.
Is it too much to ask for?

Zoë Mattacks (12)
Broadstone Middle School

I Had A Dream

I had a dream where there were no more wars,
No guns were sold to anyone.

Animals could roam free like we can,
No one could shoot them or hurt them.

All the world could have access to water,
No people would die of thirst.

No litter could be chucked on the floor,
You couldn't make the streets look a mess.

No humans could murder others,
No robbers could take people's belongings.

There was no more poverty,
No children starving or dying.

But the biggest thing of all,
Everyone would have a happy life.

Ben Moyse (12)
Broadstone Middle School

Dreaming

I walked down the street expecting the normal beggars
Who are ill and lonely.

But everyone is looking happy,
There is no sign of ill people or poor.

There's no litter or gum on the pavement,
Everyone is happy.

How is it that yesterday everything was different?
I must be dreaming.
I went into a hospital,
There were no injured or unwell people there.

There was no fighting,
No people smoking.

Finally, there is peace in the world.

Jez Atkin (11)
Broadstone Middle School

I Had A Dream

I dreamt,
Poverty never existed,
Everyone was equal,
Nothing was ever wasted,
I dreamt of my world,
I dreamt of happiness.

I dreamt,
No war was ever created,
No bullet would leave a gun,
Words became meaningful,
A bloody, battered corpse would never be found,
I dreamt of my world,
I dreamt of happiness.

I dreamt,
No racism,
Black and white could mix,
Faiths and religions could join,
Differences didn't matter.
I dreamt of my world,
I dreamt of happiness.

I dreamt,
No one made pollution,
We could all breathe fresh, clean air,
Global warming wasn't dangerous,
Crazy cars were nowhere to be seen.
I dreamt of my world,
I dreamt of happiness.

Jessica Girvin (11)
Broadstone Middle School

Dream

I have a dream,
That everybody is free,
That no one is in poverty
And there is world peace.

I have a dream,
That there is no waste,
That there is no pollution
And animals are free.

I have a dream,
That everybody has food,
That everybody has water
And everybody is happy.

I have a dream,
That energy isn't worth money,
That cars run on electricity,
So I can be happy.
That is my dream.

Alex Fair (12)
Broadstone Middle School

I Have A Dream

I have a dream of a world
With no racism and no poverty.

I have a dream where people don't get bullied
For what's wrong with them and cannot do.

I have a dream
With no stalking and perverts.

I have a dream where black and white citizens
Get along with each other.

I have a dream.

Alex Huntley (12)
Broadstone Middle School

My Dreams

In my dreams I imagine
A world with no diseases and great quality medical technology.
In my dreams I imagine
A world with no wars, no conflicts or bloody battles.
In my dreams I imagine
A world without poverty or starving people.
In my dreams I imagine
A world of happiness and peace where people have fun.
In my dreams I imagine
A world of equality and joy.
In my dreams I imagine
A world of rich people with no greed or lust for power.
In my dreams I imagine
A world of no waste.
In my dreams I imagine
A world of freedom, free from all bad things.
In my dreams I imagine
A world of only good things, unharmed by evil.
In my dreams I imagine
A world where animals roam freely without worry of extinction.
In my dreams I imagine
A world of no forced labour.
In my dreams I imagine
A world of no deserts where people die, starving and forgotten.

Matt Copp (13)
Broadstone Middle School

My Dream

I had a dream where there were no more street fights
And no one hurt each other anymore.

I had a dream where no one made you pay
For the smallest things.

I had a dream where no one took someone's bag
Or money, for fun.

I had a dream where everyone was treated the same,
With respect and kindness.

I had a dream where everyone had their own piece of land
And everyone made it exactly how they wanted it to be.

I had a dream where there was no vandalising
Of other people's property.

I dreamt of a world with lots of animals
And no poachers to kill them.

Mark Sandford (11)
Broadstone Middle School

My Dream!

My dream has no hate, no people ranting and raving.
My dream has no war, no innocent people dying.
My dream has more freedom, so much free spirit.
My dream has no poverty, no sad faces crying out.
My dream has peace, so joyful people are.
My dream has no crime, no badness and sin.
My dream has no white or black, neither anger,
Just happiness all around.
The people will work together as one,
Helping and comforting.
All shall be equal, no higher authority.
People will treat others how they would like to be treated.
Religion will make no difference between friends or families.
My dream could be real if people would just give it a go
And just try!

Benjamin Judge (12)
Broadstone Middle School

I Have A Dream

I have a dream:
A dream that the homeless live in mansions
                            and so does everyone else.
I have a dream:
A dream that everyone lives in harmony.
I have a dream:
A dream that no one goes hungry.
I have a dream:
A dream that everyone is rich.
I have a dream:
A dream that black and white people live in peace.
I have a dream:
A dream that no one gets hurt.
I have a dream:
A dream that everyone is happy.
I have a dream:
A dream that no one will die alone.
I have a dream:
A dream that there's no prisons.
I have a dream:
A dream that all races and creeds respect each other.
I have a dream.

Gary Brushett (13)
Broadstone Middle School

My Dream

I have a dream,
That animals are free,
From suffering and illness.

I have a dream,
That everyone is included,
Not excluded because of colour or race.

I have a dream,
That everyone is happy,
Not beaten, or upset from unhappiness.

I have a dream,
That no one is poor,
Everyone had enough food and money to live.

I have a dream,
That the air was fresh and clean,
Not ruined by pollution and carelessness.

I have a dream,
That all my dreams would come true,
For a better future of happiness and pleasure.

That's my dream.
How about you?

Alexandra Hughes (12)
Broadstone Middle School

My Dream

I had a dream that was fantastic
I had a dream that was amazing
I had a dream that would make the world
How it was meant to be.

I dreamt people would live longer
No poverty
I dreamt no global warming
No crime either.

I dreamt an explosion
Of all the sins in the world
I dreamt the world was perfect
No more hunger or pain.

I had a dream that was fantastic
I had a dream that was amazing
I had a dream that would make the world
How it was meant to be.

Oscar Borton (11)
Broadstone Middle School

I Have A Dream

I had a dream,
My dream is this.
That no person in the world will be killed,
The world will be a peaceful place.

I had a second dream and it went something like this:
Everyone in the world will have education,
They will be clever and smart,
Go to college too.

My last dream is this:
The world will be generous and kind,
There would be no need for police stations, prisons or courts,
The world will be fair, safe and sound,
This is a dream, a dream of mine.

Samantha Bumford (13)
Broadstone Middle School

A Dream World

A world should be free
And so should the people and animals in it.
Imagine a world,
A world where the people can have a say on the new laws,
Where animals can roam freely,
Where there are no prisons.

A world should be clean.
Imagine a world,
A world where the streets are clean and smooth,
Where people don't have to pick up other people's litter and rubbish,
Where there isn't any pollution.

A world should be kind and so should the people in it.
Imagine a world,
A world where people don't vandalise parks,
Where everybody respects each other.

Why can't it be our world?

Jack Durham (11)
Broadstone Middle School

I Had A Dream

I had a dream I think you'll understand
I would like to tell you about it, if I can
I was walking through the 'Promised Land'
Meeting people I didn't know, shaking their hand
But I didn't know what I was doing
Thinking who are these people? Where am I?
What am I doing here and why am I shaking your hand?
Then I realised I was in a heavy place
Where all the sad people go when they are down.
I must be down, I don't know, it is all confusing.
So then, why can't I come down? I am happy now.
The next day I woke up and it was all just a silly dream.

Bethanie Gomm (12)
Broadstone Middle School

Imagine A World

The words I speak are from the heart,
I had a dream of a better world with peace and happiness,
Everyone is equal, there is no black or white,
Only peace and harmony.

The words I speak are from the heart,
In my world there are no guns,
No killing, no taking innocent lives,
There is no sin, only hope.

The words I speak are from the heart,
In my world there is nothing but beauty and art,
No graffiti plaguing lives,
No rubbish littering lives,
But most of all, there will be no wars,
No bombing, no hurting or being bad,
In my world there is only good.

Come, let's make this dream come true,
Because it will surely help me and *you.*

Conner Ross-Read (12)
Broadstone Middle School

A Better World

A better world where violence, drugs and racism doesn't exist
A better world where the homeless live in houses
A better world where poor families have food and money
A better world where crimes are only a myth
A better world where anger and fear does not exist
A better world where wars are a game on the PlayStation.

Ashley Jacobs (12)
Broadstone Middle School

I Had A Dream!

I had a dream.

I dreamed that there was no rich or poor,
Everyone was equal.

The schools had no bullies, the children all got on,
They never had arguments or fights.

I had a dream.

There was no such thing as Hell,
Heaven was the only place.

I had a dream.

There was no racism on the streets, whatever colour you are,
Any religion, it didn't matter.

I had a dream.

The weather was always good,
The sun was shining bright and it never rained.
The weather was so good, all day, every day.

I had a dream!

Cassie Marshall (13)
Broadstone Middle School

I Have A Dream

I have a dream,
A dream of peace and happiness.
I have a dream,
A dream of freedom and free will.
I have a dream,
A dream of fun and education.
I have a dream,
A dream of human rights and freedom.

Jonathan Arnekleiv (12)
Broadstone Middle School

In My Dream

In my dream,
I would like
No wars, where people fight.

In my dream,
I would like
Peace for everyone,
Where no one has anger.

In my dream,
I would like
No murders,
Where people have an unknown urgency
And want to hurt others.

In my dream,
I would like
No thieves,
Where people snatch things
And run before they get caught.

In my dream,
I would like
Green, grassy fields,
Full of happiness.

Eloise Towning (11)
Broadstone Middle School

My Dream

My dream is for animals
All weak and small
The ones in the zoos
I don't see love or care, but pain in all.

Their fear of poachers
And hunters too
The big booby traps all over the bush
Which strike them down with a huge, loud *crash*
Blood pours out
Like water from a spout
And they lick their wounds
Like a child with a lolly.

My dream is for animals
All weak and small
The ones in the zoos
I don't see love or care, but pain in all
     And that's *my* dream for animals!

Alex Cox (11)
Broadstone Middle School

Imagine

I have a dream
Where the world is clean.

I have a vision
Where I like division.

I have a feel
Of something real.

I have a dream
Where the world can gleam.

I imagine.

Drew Giggins (11)
Broadstone Middle School

I Once Had A Dream!

I once had a dream
And in my dream I saw the world was a better place
We would forget about war
And no one would get hurt,
We would all get along
I once had a dream.

I once had a dream
And in my dream I heard children playing in the playground
Happily, without fighting or bullying
All children sounded the same
All equal and happy
I once had a dream.

I once had a dream
And in my dream we looked and had the same
No one had more than others
And no one had less
We would all get along
I once had a dream.

I once had a dream
And in my dream I heard small animals
Hopping and leaping through the grass
The small insects crawling through the mud
Like army soldiers at war
I once had a dream.

Emily Worssell (12)
Broadstone Middle School

My Dream

In my dream world there would be no wars,
There would be no hunger,
Everyone would be peaceful.

In my world
In my dream teachers don't nag,
Classrooms aren't like prison cells!

In my own little dream world,
I am free as the kestrel,
Soaring in the sky.

Desks don't chain me,
Money does not weight me down,
I am able to walk away.

In my dream world,
There will be no anger,
There will be no racism.

In my little world of my own,
There will be no fighting,
No violence.

Nick Phelps (12)
Broadstone Middle School

In My World

In my world
There is no work
In my world
There is no anger
Everyone is free.

In my world
Robots make money
In my world
Everyone has a friend

In my world
There would be
A pool of fried fish
And a cup of BBQ sauce
In everyone's garden.

Joe Shackleton (13)
Broadstone Middle School

I Had A Dream

In my dream I would stop poverty and hunger,
War would stop,
In my dream there would be more people
Helping each other.

In my dream world I'd give poor countries
Clean water to drink and farming crops,
Homeless people would have safe places to sleep at night.

In my dream people would respect each other
And treat each other with care.
In my dream racism would stop,
People stealing from each other would stop
And everyone would live in peace and harmony.

Ben Evans (13)
Broadstone Middle School

The Dream I Saw

I dreamt of a peaceful world,
The country a restful place,
Birds in the trees singing,
The river rushing calmly by.

The trees swaying gently,
In the cool, balmy wind,
The world was free,
There were no poachers to kill the animals.

Poverty was ended,
The world was a war-free zone,
No racism was around,
Black and white together as happy friends.

I dreamt of a peaceful world,
The country a restful place,
Birds in the trees singing,
The river rushing calmly by.

Jonathan Sparks (12)
Broadstone Middle School

My Utopia

Why can't there be a world
Without guns, without wars and war planes?
Why can't the world be a peaceful place,
Where everyone gets along?

Imagine a world without terrorism,
Without burglars, without robbers
And without murderers.

We have to do something.

I have a dream
That there are no bad things happening on Earth.
Maybe you can help my dream come true?

Bradley Ripley (10)
Broadstone Middle School

I Had A Dream

I had a dream
Of a perfect world
Where everyone got along
I had a dream

I had a dream
Where there were no racists
No nasty comments
I had a dream

I had a dream
Where there was no bullying
No fights
I had a dream

I had a dream
Where there was no poverty
No poor or rich people
I had a dream

I had a dream
Where there was no child abuse
No rapists
I had a dream.

Grace Tyror (13)
Broadstone Middle School

In My Dream

In my dream
There is no hunger around,
The world is a fairer place.

In my dream
People will not hate each other
Or use guns to kill and maim.

In my dream
The sun will be shining
And there will be no dark.

In my dream
The winters will be snowy
And the summers will be hot.

In my dream
There are no rich people or poor
As the money is all shared.

In my dream
Everything is perfect

But that was only a dream.

Ryan Quick (12)
Broadstone Middle School

Make A Difference

I made a difference once,
I made a difference by helping somebody across the road,
I made a difference when I gave some money to a poor person,
I made a difference.

I made a difference once,
I made a difference by being polite,
I made a difference when I saved my snake's life,
I made a difference.

I made a difference once,
I made a difference by standing up against poverty,
I made a difference when I worked for the police
I made a difference.

I can make a difference,
My actions, like single drops of rain,
When combined with the dreams of others,
Can make a desert bloom.

I made a difference once,
I made a difference by making the world a better place.

John Fessey (12)
Broadstone Middle School

Dream

In my dream I saw myself winning the F1 Ferrari final.
In my dream I heard the whizzing wonders of space.
In my dream it smelt of death.
In my dream I woke up in a war.
In my dream I wished that weapons did not exist.
In my dream I owned the world's largest chocolate factory.
In my dream I wished for no more poverty.
In my dream I saw myself fighting a vicious, ice-breathing dragon.
In my dream I saw myself walking along with the sea rushing
                                                through my feet.
In my dream I thought that everybody should be equal.
In my dream anything is possible.

Thomas Pearce (12)
Broadstone Middle School

My Perfect world

In my perfect world:
There is no difference between black and white,
Christian or Buddhists.

In my perfect world:
There is no difference between old and young,
Feeble and healthy.

War is no more,
Children do not work in factories.

In my perfect world:
There is no robbing,
There is no stealing.

In my perfect world:
Animals live in peace with humans
And there is no global warming.

War is no more,
Children do not work in factories.

Adam Denison (13)
Broadstone Middle School

In A Perfect World

In a perfect world . . . stop pollution
In a perfect world . . . stop murdering
In a perfect world . . . there should be peace
In a perfect world . . . stop children crying.

In a perfect world . . . stop racism
In a perfect world . . . stop wars
In a perfect world . . . stop shoplifting
In a perfect world . . . stop slamming doors.

In a perfect world . . . there will be no more animal cruelty
In a perfect world . . . there will be no more police
In a perfect world . . . there will be no more wars
In a perfect world . . . there will be peace.

Ruby Bissagar (11)
Broadstone Middle School

I Had A Dream

I had a dream,
Where the world
Was a wonderful place to live
People were all so happy
No one got hurt.

I had a dream,
Where everyone was so kind
Caring for each other
It was a wonderful place to be.

I had a dream,
Where there were lots of animals
Running free in the long grass.

I had a dream,
Where the sun was scorching hot
People were lying on the beach
Dolphins jumping up and down
In the sparkling turquoise sea.

I had a dream,
Where everyone got the same amount of everything
Everyone went to school
And got good jobs that they wanted.

Elizabeth Smart (13)
Broadstone Middle School

I Have A Dream

I have a dream,
A vision for the future.

I have a dream for the world,
The world blood painted red,
The world jealousy turned green,
The world hatred torn apart.

A dream where
The world's war, murder and pain
Have long since been forgotten
And we are all as one.

But the reality is harsh,
Children are buried under rubble,
The parents screaming names,
Names, of the dead.

Disease, hunger, famine
In the poverty-stricken countries,
They can't cure,
No food to eat.

When will my dream come true?

Fiona Bustard (12)
Broadstone Middle School

Imagine

Think:
Think of the world as a better place
Or
Think of a world with poverty
And the Earth a junkyard of waste.

See:
See the children begging for food
Or
See the children thanking for food.

Touch:
Touch the fur of an animal's coat
And feel it shivering with fear and fright and as dark as night
Or
Touch its fur, silky, smooth, warm and light.

Hear:
Hear people screaming as bombs are being dropped
Or
Hear the people laughing without stopping.

My dream is a utopia world,
Hearing the birds singing
As
The children are swinging.

I have a dream,
My utopia world.

Charlotte Durant (11)
Broadstone Middle School

I Have A Dream

Imagine,
A wonderful world,
Where children from all around the world,
Go to school.

Imagine,
An amazing Earth,
Where no wars break out
And everything is peaceful.

Imagine,
Peaceful places,
Where everyone gets on with each other,
Peaceful, peaceful, peaceful.

Imagine,
The world free from poverty,
Where people say yes
To education.

Imagine,
A glorious Earth,
Where people say no to drugs
And alcohol.

Imagine,
A wonderful world,
Where the Earth is not polluted
And the rich help the poor.

Suzanna French (12)
Broadstone Middle School

I Had A Dream

I had a dream,
Where the poor,
Were not poor,
Where poverty was made history
And friends were not lost.

I had a dream,
Where evil,
Turned to good,
Where no one killed each other
And there was peace on Earth.

I had a dream,
Where the hungry,
Were not hungry,
Where people were not enemies
And there was joy in the world.

I had a dream,
Where people who were sad,
Were happy,
Where black and white people were equal
And there was hope on Earth.

I had a dream,
Where all,
Was not lost,
Where religion did not matter
And there was happiness on Earth.

I had a dream,
Where the withered hand,
Was not gone,
Where death did not matter
And there was no sadness on the Earth.

I had a dream,
Where the thirsty,
Were not thirsty,
Where love never broke
And there was love on Earth again.

I had a dream,
Where I changed the world,
For the better,
It was a better world,
As they listened to one voice.

Meg Selby (12)
Broadstone Middle School

Imagine

Think about the future . . .
Hear the screams of children
As the bombs are dropped.
Hear the peaceful wind in the trees.
See the sun shining bright in the sky.
Consider a world without war.
Smell the food cooking,
Touch the clean floor.
Think of a world without racism.
Hear the whispering of children
That could change the world.
See the yummy cakes
Sitting on the side of the counter.
I have a dream that the world will be a better place.
Consider a whole new world.
Hear the jingling of the keys in the pocket.
Think of the yummy chocolate cakes.
See beautiful cats roaming around on the green grass,
Instead of war.

Brittany French (11)
Broadstone Middle School

My Perfect World

Consider no wars:
Would it mean more people or not?
Would there be so many bloodthirsty countries?
Imagine no more gunshots waking you at night.

Imagine a world filled with kinder people:
Think about all the dying children being saved,
Just in the nick of time.
See all the starving faces turn happy,
Hear all the moaning and groaning turn silent.

Think of a delightful, blue sky
Turning as black as a witch's heart
Because of *pollution!*
Think of money-rattling pockets;
Suddenly it disappears to only the amount they need.
The rest goes to the poor and needy.

Think of Africa,
One of the poorest continents;
A lot of countries in poverty.
There are people starving to death.
Will we sit around doing nothing?

It is sad but it's not necessary.
You could donate money to charities.
There are many people dying
As *you* read this poem.
You can change that immediately!

Adam Stroud (11)
Broadstone Middle School

I Have A Dream

Some dream of royalty,
Some dream of money,
But I don't dream for myself,
I think about bringing peace to the world.

Some dream of cars,
Some dream of mansions,
But I don't want possessions,
I want pollution to cease and the air to be clean.

Some dream of fame,
Some dream of fortune,
But I only want to help
And put a stop to poverty.

Some dream of marriage,
Some dream of children,
But I can't think of that,
Until all the guns are silenced and war is put to an end.

Some dream of power,
Some dream of glory,
But I dream of happiness
And love being spread to everyone.

Some dream for themselves,
But my dreams are for the world.

Deborah Smith (13)
Broadstone Middle School

I Have A Dream

I dream that we have no war
Cos I just can't take it anymore
And we only fight for education
And the children.

I dream that we live in unison
As power of one
And we respect each other
And our religion.

I dream that we know
That you can change the world
By changing yourself
So let's change.

Just dream like me, take action!
Then one will follow you
Then one will follow the other one
Next thing you know
You've got a billion!

I dream.

Kate Hennessy (13)
Broadstone Middle School

They Say

They say world hunger will stop
They say terrorism numbers will drop
They say they'll cut down on under age drinking,
They say they'll get criminals thinking.

They say, they say . . .

But actions speak louder than words
Or so they say.

Kathryn Pritchard (10)
Broadstone Middle School

My Perfect Earth

I have a dream,
That is close to my heart,
In which eyes will have no tears;
Mouths will be empty of scolding
And slaps will have no smart.

Peace will reign over the Earth,
The guns will be stilled and poverty will be no more,
This Earth will be cherished
And global warming will have been forgotten;
This Earth will have no unjust law.

On the perfect Earth everyone would be equal,
No more would there be robbers or crooks;
Money would be of no value
And everyone would give and share their goods.

This Earth would never have heard of famine or drought.
Every disease would be cured,
On my glorious Earth.

This is my perfect dream!

Rachael Paton (12)
Broadstone Middle School

Imagine

Imagine . . . a world of peace,
But imagine . . . the fighting.

Think . . . a bright blue sky,
But consider . . . a land of pollution.

Feel . . . the calm seawater,
But feel . . . a sea of rubbish.

Smell . . . the clean air,
But smell . . . the dead fish.

Hear . . . the birds singing,
But hear . . . the silence.

Dominic Wood (11)
Broadstone Middle School

I Have A Dream

In my dream,
A new world is created,
Where racism is an unknown word
And crying is never heard.

In my dream,
Rainforests are full of life
And no fumes clog lungs.

In my dream,
Wars are never started
And guns are cast away.

In my dream,
Evil drugs are never taken
And competitive sports are just for fun.

In my dream,
The homeless are given homes
And everyone is equal.

In my dream,
Factories are replaced with fields of flowers
And happiness is spread throughout the world.

Natasha Underwood (12)
Broadstone Middle School

Imagine

In a perfect world things will all go well,
No pollution or horrid smell.

In a perfect world big factories will disappear,
Lovely flowers will reappear.

In a perfect world no wars or terrorist attacks,
Chewing gum will not be spat.

In a perfect world no under age drinking,
We will get criminals thinking!

James Carter (11)
Broadstone Middle School

I Have A Dream

In my dream I see the world at its best.
Wars are gone with the wind
And the hand of friendship is spread over the land,
And with this there is peace.

I dream.

Skin colour is just two colours
And these two colours can unite to make a better world.
Racism is washed away by the rain.

I dream.

The air is clean,
Pollution is gone,
The natural world
Is peaceful once more.

I dream.

Poverty is an unknown thing
And it is something that no one in any part of the world
Needs to worry about or deal with.

These are my dreams about the world.

Emily King-Underwood (13)
Broadstone Middle School

I Dream Of A World

I dream of a world so healthy that the poor will never starve again.
I dream of a world so kind that people never knew how to say and do
horrid things.
I dream of a world so colourful that the streets will put smiles on
everyone's faces.
I dream of a world so free that you wouldn't have to work.
I dream of a world so magical that the stars in children's eyes would
light up the night.
This was my special dream of what a beautiful world it could be.

Megan King (11)
Broadstone Middle School

A Dreamy World!

We all dream,
But if only they came true,
The world would be such a good place,
For me and you!
Birds could be free to fly,
But why,
Can't we all get along?

We all dream,
But if only they came true
And everybody was equal,
Like me and you!
It does not matter what we look like,
If we are black or if we are white.

We all dream,
If you made your dreams come true,
What a peaceful world it would be,
For me and you!

Rio-Taya Courtenay-Lewis (11)
Broadstone Middle School

I Wish

Imagine
Making a difference;
Imagine
The racist comments never being said,
Imagine
Being helped by the opposite colour,
Imagine
Nobody caring about your skin colour,
Imagine
Black and white mixing,
Imagine
The hand of friendship having no colour.
Imagine.

Ben Hutton (12)
Broadstone Middle School

I Have A Dream

I have a dream where the sun always shines
Where there are no fights or wars.
I have a dream where everyone is friends
And no one is mean to anyone.

I have a dream where there is no death
And no global warming.
I have a dream where there is no pollution
But cars can drive around.

I have a dream where there is no hunting
Just to get some animal fur.
I have a dream where there are no zoos
And animals can roam free in their natural habitats.

I have a dream where everybody is equal
And no one is the same.

Jack Clements (11)
Broadstone Middle School

Dream

I dream of a world where the poor become rich
And poverty disappears.

I dream of a world where the birds can fly free
And the trees are let be.

And I dream and I dream!

I dream of a world where the sun always shines
And the animals can live a happy life.

I dream of a world where colour isn't judged
And black and white are equal!

And I dream and I dream!

If we all work together, our dreams can come true
And I know you and me want it too!

Lauren Ayers (12)
Broadstone Middle School

How I Dream Of The World

I dream of a world where,
People can live together,
No worries about their colour,
For all people to be able to speak,
Without anger taking over.

I dream of a world where,
Animals are not killed,
Not hunted, not disturbed,
For them to wander in the wilderness,
Without running away from fear.

I dream of a world where,
There is peace,
No rage or anger, no running away,
For everyone to be together,
Without danger or harm near.

That is how I dream the world could be.

Hannah Newey (11)
Broadstone Middle School

I Have A Dream

I have a dream,
Where nobody can ever be mean.

I have a dream,
To see animals set free forever
And never be treated badly.

I have a dream,
That I shall help animals in all ways
And be keen.

I have a dream,
To see the world changed by humans
To the way it was.

Carys Digby (11)
Broadstone Middle School

A Perfect World

I have a vision of a perfect world
Where black children play with white children
Where there is no such thing as poverty
And everyone is equal.

I have a vision of a perfect world
Where everyone has clean water
And access to medical aid
And where people have enough to eat.

I have a vision of a perfect world
Where skin colour doesn't matter
And everyone has employment
Where every child has school.

I have a vision of a perfect world
Where there are no wars
And people do not fight
That is my perfect world.

Joseph Cross (12)
Broadstone Middle School

I Have A Dream

I have a dream,
A very good dream,
With no racism
And food for all,
With poverty a myth
And pollution a legend,
Where evil is a fable
And peace is the only way of life.
I had a dream,
A very good dream.

Tom Brophy (12)
Broadstone Middle School

I Have A Dream

I have a dream,
That there are no bombs, no bullets,
No suicide, no racism, no hate,
That these things don't exist.

I have a dream,
That there is harmony, that there is peace,
That there is forgiveness, that there is justice,
That these things exist and are everywhere.

I have a dream,
That white shares with black, touching, embracing,
That religions love, not hate, being friendly to each other,
That there is water in a drought
And light in the dark.

But why?
Why does the world not change?
Why are there shadowy figures?
Murderers, bombers, terrorists that choke and blind,
Devouring the world.

Why this when we could live in peace?
In a place where your colour, religion, race, wouldn't matter.

I dream of a world like this,
We should have a world like this.

Josh Perren (12)
Broadstone Middle School

Change The World

We can change the world,
Stop all the wars,
Bring peace to all,
Think!

We can change the world,
Stop the racism,
Believe in everyone's religion,
Think!

We can change the world,
Stop global warming,
We can make the world,
A better place.
Think!
Act now!

Hayley Cornish (13)
Broadstone Middle School

I Have A Dream

I have a dream
That people will wake up
And there will be peace on Earth
No diseases, no murders
Just peace.

Animals will live in harmony with humans
No wars will go on around us
And people can walk the streets of towns
Without fear of gangs.

The bullied will not get bullied anymore
And the poor will have homes
The rich will give to the poor
And we will all live together
Like a family.

Abigail Wassell (11)
Broadstone Middle School

I Had A Dream

I had a dream that would change the world,
Where the poor had money
And the hungry had food.

I had a dream that would change the world,
Where everyone was equal,
No matter their race or religion.

I had a dream that would change the world,
Where even the deadliest, deserted deserts,
Provided water for all.

I had a dream that would change the world,
Where I saw the hand reach out for the pen,
That would sign for world peace.

I had a dream that would change the world,
Where neighbour got along with neighbour
And brother got along with sister.

I had a dream that would change the world,
Where there were no wars or fights,
Where no one got hurt.

I had a dream that would change the world.

Emily Parsons (12)
Broadstone Middle School

I Have A Dream

I dream of a world,
Where the birds fly freely,
Where mixed race children happily play,
Under a sandy-gold sun,
Dainty flower petals flitter in a cool breeze,
Like a beautiful blue butterfly,
Its sapphire wings fluttering gracefully through the sky.

I dream of people,
Who care for one another.
People that respect different religions
And don't tease about people's looks.
People that have consideration for each other
And only see unkindness in their darkest dreams.

I dream of a world,
Full of joyful people.
Pretty wildlife covering the Earth's surface,
People that don't have to worry about their skin,
Children that don't worry about going to school.
I have a dream.

Ellie Hilborne (11)
Broadstone Middle School

I Had A Vision Once

I had a vision once -
It showed the world at peace,
Huddled in a glaze of light,
Vanquishing evil from afar,
That is my vision.

My vision shows a world of equality,
No matter the colour of a person's skin,
Or the pennies in his hand.

The vision is not just of men, but of animals,
They deserve as much of our planet as we do.
No more ivory hunts or poachers,
Who kill for something as common as money.
Would we be happy and joyful if we were hunted?

This vision also showed people working together,
Helping each other to stop the violence throughout the world,
No matter what your religion.

I had a vision once,
It showed the world at peace,
Huddled in a glaze of light,
Vanquishing evil from afar,
That is my vision.

Connor Hallisey (11)
Broadstone Middle School

My Dream

The Earth is a withered flower.
I dream . . .
I dream of a world with no pain,
Where people have no right to fight,
Where guns are destroyed and melted,
Where bullets and knives are melted, destroyed, bent and broken,
Where there is no fear.
I dream.

I dream . . .
I dream of a world not soured by evil,
Where race and religion mean nothing,
Where war and bloodshed are banished.
I dream.

I dream . . .
I dream of a world not poisoned by greed,
And people farm together,
Where the environment is kept beautiful,
Where material possessions don't matter.
I dream.

Oliver Smith (11)
Broadstone Middle School

I Wish Upon Miracles

I wish upon a miracle
There be peace between countries
And human beings.

I wish upon a miracle
I could hear laughter
Not a million tears.

I wish upon a miracle
I could see poverty
Disappearing.

I wish upon a miracle
That we can't hear the cries
Of the helpless.

I wish upon a miracle
I could see children
Not going hungry.

I wish upon a miracle
I could see and hear
Miracles happening in the world.

I wish upon a miracle
To look upon the world
And see it change.

I wish upon a miracle
We won't give up
We'll carry on.

Lauren Trent (10)
Broadstone Middle School

I Have A Dream

Look at the world we're killing,
Look at the world, it's weeping.
    I have a dream
That there are no more wars,
That people get along,
    I have a dream.

    I have a dream
That poverty does not exist,
That the environment is clean,
    I have a dream.

Look at the world, it's weeping,
Look at the blood we're spilling.
    I have a dream
That animals roam freely,
That there is clean, fresh water,
    I have a dream.

    I have a dream
That alcoholic drinking stops,
That people don't smoke
    I have a dream.

Look at the blood we're spilling,
Look at the world we're killing.

    I have a dream . . .
        Well, I had a dream.

Stevie Addicott (13)
Broadstone Middle School

I Dream

I dream of a world that is peaceful,
A world without wars.
I dream of a world where everyone is friends,
They would have no enemies or hatred towards one another
And they would reach out their hands to help.
I dream of a world without killing or stealing,
No one would die of unnatural causes.
I dream of a world where everyone is loved,
Each and every one of us would have a warm, cosy home to go to.
I dream of a world where everyone respects other people's religions
and races,
Racism wouldn't exist,
Everyone would play happily together no matter what colour.
I dream of a world without poachers or animal killing,
Every living creature would be treated as you would like to be.

Everyone knows that the world can't be perfect,
But imagine if this could really happen,
You can help it come true!

Eleanor Pilborough (11)
Broadstone Middle School

I Have A Dream

I have a dream, a dream where there are doves flying across the sky,
Across the beaches and seas, soaring through trees of green,
I have a dream, a dream where the people who are homeless find a
warm home,
And for the people who are hungry to be fed.
I have a dream, a dream where black and white are equal
And for them to gather strength to bring peace between one another.
I have a dream, a dream where the animals who are being tested,
Are set free to go back to their natural habitat.
I have a dream, a dream where the streets stay clean
And people's property is respected,
Where windows are not being busted and doors are not being kicked.
I have a dream, a dream where the world is a better place.

Becky Troke (12)
Broadstone Middle School

I Have A Dream

My dream of the world
Would be happiness in every household,
Each smile a ray of sunshine,
Each day full of fun.
Fairness in each village,
Each town, each nation,
When there is fairness in each nation,
There is peace in the world.
I dream of the day
When we are treated as equal,
The young, the old, the shy and the bold.
I dream that each person is safe and sound
And that no one is sleeping on the ground.
I dream that the animals
Are not hunted or killed,
So that people's selfish fun is filled.
I dream of the day when there is no war,
When everyone obeys the law,
When everyone has a heart and a home,
When no one feels they are all alone.

Rebecca Matcham (12)
Broadstone Middle School

In My Dream

My dream is no one has to live in poverty
And there is eternal peace in every corner of the world.
The government is equal to everyone else
Then maybe we could make our own decisions.
In my dream people could live
Without fear of crime or disease,
And God's Ten Commandments were the only laws.
Also in my dream I saw that there was no pollution or landfills
And there were forests thick as jungles instead.
That is my dream.
What's yours?

Elliot Talbot (11)
Broadstone Middle School

I Have A Dream

The truth is twisted,
Buried and blurred,
The lying ones own
Not what they deserve
Riots and bombs,
Soldiers fight,
Not for what they believe,
Not for what's right.
The innocent are tortured,
By their suffering and pain,
They scream but no one hears them,
The guilty are to blame.
Crashing and crumbling,
Nature seeks revenge,
Half our constant battle,
That never seems to end.
My dreams lie shattered and broken,
I look around me,
No one has yet spoken,
Of the horrors in our world!

Sam Essam (11)
Broadstone Middle School

I Have A Dream

I have a dream
A dream unimaginable to life
A dream that has no point being dreamt.

I have a dream
That poverty is just a thought
That famine and drought is all in our heads.

I have a dream
That the world is my ally
And wars are only in games.

I have a dream
Where water is our fuel
And pollution is a thing from the past.

I have a dream
A dream unimaginable to life
A dream that has no point being dreamt.

Anya Levkouskis (13)
Broadstone Middle School

My Icon Called George Best

Football is my passion,
Football is my joy,
I've been kicking footballs,
Ever since I was a boy.

Nothing makes me happier,
Than pursuing my life's quest,
To be as good if possible,
As my icon called George Best.

He truly was a master,
In the art of ball control,
Magnificent to watch,
The team's heart and soul.

The fans' eyes never left him,
You would have been impressed,
When he scored all the goals,
My icon called George Best.

When he ran he was amazing,
He was faster than the rest,
I really wish I'd seen him,
My icon called George Best.

Idolised by millions,
He really had been blessed,
The owner of two magic feet,
My icon called George Best.

Gregory Perkins (12)
Broadstone Middle School

I Dream . . .

I dream of a world where . . .

There are no wars or protests
The world should be at peace

I hope that everybody will soon have
A good supply of food and water
No one should starve

There should be no racist comments
Everyone is unique
But we are all human

There should be no bullying
We should all treat others
How we would like to be treated ourselves

There should be no abuse
Why harm others?
Think before you act

Just stop, think
Happiness should be everywhere.

Charlotte Roberts (12)
Broadstone Middle School

Imagine

Imagine a key,
That would unlock a perfect
World.

A clear blue sea,
With non-polluted
Waters.

Imagine a doorway,
That leads to a
Utopia.

Imagine the day,
It opens up to the
World.

Imagine,
Peace, righteousness and no more
Badness.

Imagine,
A perfect
World.

Emily Phillips (11)
Broadstone Middle School

Imagine

In the future
There will be a war,
In the future
There will be no law.

In the future
Cute dogs are out,
And guns are
Out and about.

In the future
Guns are fired,
In the future
No person is hired.

In the future
People will see wounds,
In the future
People are running like baboons.

A utopia will be
Different . . .
Something like this
I consider.

A utopia
Where everybody cares
A utopia where
All trade is fair.

A utopia
Where no man is sick
A utopia
Where loads of cute dogs lick.

A utopia
Where there are no drugs
Where no one is called
A mug.

Chantelle Evans (11)
Broadstone Middle School

Dreams

I think it's important to have dreams.
My dreams are ones I hope to accomplish.
What's the point in living when you don't enjoy it?
Don't forget the importance of life . . .
Always stay happy.
I want to aim high and never give up,
Never forget the people I love
And most importantly,
Always have dreams.
No dream is impossible,
If you try and believe.

Laura Tenwick (14)
Bryanston School

My Dream

When I am older
I want to sing,
To fly sky-high
And taste the wind.
I want people to know my name,
I want to live a life of fame.
I want to be up in the stars,
A showbiz life
Surreal and fast.

But I also want my music
To create a feeling,
To help those people
Most in needing.
I want my voice to sing
Loud and clear,
To boost a person's confidence
And
Take away their fear.

I want my songs
To help people when
They're down,
To take away that lonely frown.
I want my parents to be proud,
To say, 'That's my girl,'
Out aloud.
I want my fans to sing along
To their favourite
Of my songs.

I hope that this dream
Deep down inside of me,
Will one day,
Maybe happen to me!

Alice Whitlock (14)
Bryanston School

My Dreams

I have dreams that I want to achieve,
Some are small and some are big,
Some may be impossible, some easy,
But I want these dreams to happen
And I am going to do what Winston Churchill said,
'Never, never, never give up'.

I want to save the world from war,
So that there can be peace.
I want to stop racism,
So that there will be no hate.
I want to stop poverty,
So that people are equal.
These are my big dreams.

I want to always have fun,
So that I am never down.
I want to explore the world,
So that I can see everything.
I want to become successful,
So that I can be happy.

These may be unachievable but,
'No dream is ever too small,
No dream is ever too big'.

Becca Scott (14)
Bryanston School

I Have A Dream

When I was younger than today
I knew not of complicated struggles.
I did not understand this game we play
Nor why the good can't always stay.

I did not know of twisted conflict
Nor thought about shallow trends.
I used to dream of fantasy flicks,
Spinning and dancing with perfect friends.

I'd walk through grassy fields,
Sit among flowers sweet-smelling,
Fight heroically in epic battles 'til the enemy yields,
Unwilling.

I'd find my true love in the streets of Paris,
Then we'd run away to mystic lands.
There we would laugh and talk, be blissfully happy,
Never letting go of one another's hand.

We'd dive into deep cleansing pools,
Where waterfalls flowed and crashed against stone.
We'd sleep in a hammock - such lovesick fools,
And I'd feel home.

But then I grew older.
I saw the world's beauty marred by filth.
I put aside my dreams in memory's folder,
Not forgotten, but it is for me to change those stars
                    I once dived through.

And in the monotony of reality, I now have a different dream:
My mind, body and soul are determined and will no longer hide.
I can't sit through life, then be forgotten when I'm gone.
I want to make a stand for the benefit of mankind!

I want to be recognised in history.
I have a dream - remember me.

Anna Moses (13)
Cranborne Middle School

Anybody In Particular

I walk home from school, always alone
No one wants to talk to me
They just want to stare because I look different
I act different
Why is this?

I get bullied now
I've been led to hollow depression
Everyone hates me because I look different
I act different
Why is this?

I haven't got much of a life
Working as a waitress
I wanted to be a star! Performing to my beloved audience
My dreams were broken by a single fist
I lost everything
Why is this?

I met someone today
He was different to everyone else
He treated me different
Like I was worth something for once
Why is this?

In love . . .
I met my true love by pouring him coffee
I realise that my life could have been anyone's
Who has been living in the shadows of negativity
I could have been happy all along
And now I am because I know I'm loved and accepted for being *me*.
I waited until someone opened their eyes to see the real colour in life
Everyone is different. We should accept others for being their
                                        unique selves
That's why.

Kelie Petterssen (13)
Cranborne Middle School

I Have A Dream

I have a dream that everyone can find this enlightening,
That everyone, no matter whom,
Can benefit from this teaching and can learn by its thinking.

Life is a gift, and so is this planet -
Treat them both with respect.
Those who do not care for life,
Think life is utterly boring
And those who think life is boring, *are* boring.

Obsession for materials is a mere ignorant, false view of life.
You can better the shaping of this world
In any clothes - without lifeless objects.
Judging others by what they own is a heartbreaking mistake
That can easily be avoided.

It takes strength and courage to be kind.
It takes absolute laziness to be nasty -
To be nasty is the scapegoat, the easy way out.
Those who are kind
Strive for better things in life,
To make a difference to the world,
For the better.

Do not question whether
What you do or what you say
Matters in life -
It does matter.

To conclude:
Embrace life as a newfound friend.
Understand her twists and turns.
Learn her way of being,
Her sense of knowing.
All in all,
Live *your* life how it is -
Not how others want it to be.

Hannah Deacon (13)
Cranborne Middle School

My Dream Poem

I'm thirteen with my whole life in front of me,
With nothing happening as far as I can see.
I've wished for lots of things during my life,
Like having a good job and maybe a wife.
I don't know what's coming.

I'm fifteen now and looking for jobs,
Maybe in kennels working with dogs.
Or in a dentist's playing with teeth,
Or in a fast food restaurant cooking some beef.
I still don't know what's coming.

I'm seventeen now and in my driving test,
I saw a man speeding, I saw him confess.
I'm going to college in a year or two,
To learn about dentistry and helping you.
I'm close to finding out what's coming.

I'm thirty now and I've got a career,
With a big house, what have I to fear?
I'm working in a dentist's making braces,
Then sticking them to people's faces.
I've nearly found out what's coming.

I'm sixty now and I'm retired,
I've done all in my life that I've desired.
However, I continue to learn,
Being a volunteer for Age Concern.
I'm even closer to finding out what's coming.

I'm eighty now and living on the edge,
The only thing I can eat is pureed veg.
I thought my life was for keeps,
Now all I hear is beep, beep, beep
      Beeeeep.

Mat Williets (13)
Cranborne Middle School

Dreams

A dream is something for you to keep,
Not something for others to destroy.
You make your own choices,
Go down your own paths.

We all wanted to be ballerinas or heroic firemen,
But as we grow,
Our childhood dreams are shattered like broken glass,
Sliding away from our grasp.

Take a risk,
Walk down the harder road,
Don't go down the one most people take,
Be confident, be free.

Leave the painful memories of the past behind you,
Make a fresh start to your life.
Don't hang onto events that should have been forgotten,
Be the outgoing youth you have had locked away inside of
                                            you for so long.

You'll only gain self happiness
If you follow through your dreams,
And come out of your shell
To live life to its true potential.

Samantha Roberts (13)
Cranborne Middle School

I Have A Dream!

I have a dream that there would be no more poverty in the world,
I have a dream that there will be no need for adverts with
children dying,
But more of the same children having a life-changing experience.

I have a dream.

I have a dream that no more children will be taken off the streets
To fight in war for Xbox material,
But instead looked after and fed.

I have a dream.

I have a dream that when I walk down the street
There will be no more homeless people there, starving.

I have a dream.

I keep asking myself
Why aren't people helping?
Well I am, but I need you to help,
To save people's lives.
Will you help?

Rebecca Withers (13)
Cranborne Middle School

Dream

I have a dream,
To do things I have never done before,
To visit extraordinary places,
With unique cuisines and famous sights,
See the world from up above,
Whilst riding in a hot air balloon,
Or swimming in the calm turquoise sea,
The sun beating down on my skin.

I have a dream,
To do one thing every day that scares me,
To jump out of an aeroplane,
Have the world spinning around me after a 9,000ft drop,
To have the fresh air around me
And breeze against my face, gravity taking me over,
Live to my heart's content, be happy, smile!

Amy Lawrence (13)
Cranborne Middle School

Dreams Are Like . . .

Dreams . . .
    Dreams are like the fluffiness of clouds,
    Seeing them, but never reaching them.
    Dreams are like a secret world
    Talking to you in a special kind of language.
    Dreams come in every shape, size and form
    But every one has some special meaning to you.
    Dreams are like a piece of string,
    You never know how long it takes to reach them.
Every dream is possible,
It's whether you really want to do it that counts.
So . . .
    Think of your dream
    Aim for your dream
    And succeed in your dream!

Katie Davies (12)
Cranborne Middle School

Chances

There are people in the world,
Who can't be bothered to make two cents
And think the world owes them a living,
Whilst every day there are people working
And studying hard to earn a living.
If they can do it, we can.
Around the world there are people
Giving back to the community and donating to others,
While celebs are swanning around,
Wasting their money on Gucci and Ferrari.
If others can do it, so can they.
Millions of children don't go to school
Because they're too poor,
If the rich people give a little back,
They would be helping a great person
Who could discover the cure for cancer?
If only we had the chance.
My dream is to make a difference,
To help people and give back
So that they can have the chances,
See the sights and fulfil their dreams.

Fiona Penny (12)
Cranborne Middle School

Dreams

What are dreams?
Dreams are what make people,
Their personality, thoughts and life.
Dreams are forgotten, real life sets in,
Reality is not what you wanted.
Dreams along with laughter and joy have gone.

You are holding back, having doubts,
Dreams, are they really possible?
So near but so far, you look up,
The finish is in your grasp.
You look down, you are shaken,
But adrenaline carries you through.

To fulfil your dream is the highest you can go,
You have to touch the sky,
Feel the clouds against your face.
Your efforts and hard work have got you there,
You feel proud and strong.
You are there, you have achieved your dream.

Holly Morgan (13)
Cranborne Middle School

Musical Dreams

I believe that music is what makes dreams come alive,
The thoughts that make the ideas flow freely into your head.
I believe that nobody is a person until their soul has come alive,
Brought alive by the way people think and the things that
others have said.
I believe that music shows someone's personality and true light,
Making how they really feel show up,
Not just in their dreams but every day in their lives.
I believe no two people are the same in any shape, size or form,
But looks are not important, it's the inside dreams that count.
The truthful dream that should be shown on the inside and out!

Georgina Towler (13)
Cranborne Middle School

Hero

Everyone's had the dream.
The dream where the world is ending.
You think: *why is the world ending?*
And then you're given a choice:
Do you sit down and wait for the final moment?
Or do you hope to the heavens that someone will do
                                        something about it?

But do we think?
Do we think that that person could ever be you?
You can pluck up the courage,
You can relight the dying embers,
You can save the world.

I had a dream, and in that dream,
I had a thought: *every generation needs a hero.*
Then I thought:
That hero could be me.

Mike Wale (13)
Cranborne Middle School

Dreams

When I was young I wanted to be
The first person to land on Mars.
When I was young I wanted to have
Hundreds of really cool cars.

When I grew up
I forgot all my dreams.
When I grew up
I knew what life really means.

Now I am older
I know what I want.
Now I am older
I know what you want.

So when you are older
Don't forget all your dreams.
When you are older
Find out what life really means.

Don't let others hold you back
Do what you want and don't go back.

Rosie Campbell (13)
Cranborne Middle School

Life!

Life is a library,
With different stories you must understand.
To receive the perfect one,
You must follow rules;
I am what I am,
I think what I think,
To me, the impossible is possible,
To see the world,
To meet new people,
Live to your heart's content,
To make the most of life,
Be yourself,
If you think and learn,
Life will be easier,
To think, you must think,
But to experience, the world is your oyster,
Now, go out there and make the most of it!

Joel Williams (12)
Cranborne Middle School

I Have A Dream

TV advertisements to advertise the new Xbox
All the children want to get it with its latest new look
To get an Xbox means children our age are killed
I have a dream that selfishness will stop.
I have a dream!
Children living the dream with a home full of comfort
Their lives are perfect with a loving family and people that care
Despite all this, some children have no home, no family or food
I have a dream that poverty will stop
I have a dream!
Does this girl have a home like me?
Does she have a loving family?
Does she have a school to learn?
Or does she work but not earn?
I have a dream!
What would the world be like without poverty?
What a different place it would be!

Lucy Sparrow (12)
Cranborne Middle School

World Without Poverty

Imagine a world where people weren't poor,
In debt and needing financial help.
I have a dream.

Imagine a world where people weren't hungry,
Dying and lying famished on the streets.
I have a dream.

Imagine a world without deadly diseases,
HIV, tuberculosis and malaria.
I have a dream.

Poverty is something we should deal with
And deal with it fast.

It's not just in Africa, it's everywhere . . .

Thomas Rodwell (11)
Lytchett Minster School

I Have A Dream

I see a place . . .
Where there's no smoking,
No drugs,
And no unnecessary deaths.

In this place . . .
I see children playing,
People laughing,
And babies' first smiles.

This place is . . .
Our world, that we live in,
That's being destroyed,
That's being polluted.
Stop!

I see a place!

Chelsea Venier (12)
Lytchett Minster School

My Dad

I'm glad my dad is my dad,
Even when he gets mad at me,
I know there's a reason.
When I do stuff, I don't try to please him,
Because I know he will be happy for me
If I just be me.

He helps me when I'm stuck,
I don't get some of the stuff he says,
But it helps me anyway.
He helps me every day
In a small way, every day.
He's made loads of stuff,
He's good at keeping junk,
But he finds uses for lots of things,
But may chuck most of it in the bin.

Liam Murray (13)
Lytchett Minster School

I Had A Dream

I had a dream,
Unlike any other,
It was about a magic bean.

And on its leaves,
Were all ideas,
Of how to help the trees.

On some it said 'Anti-pollution',
Or 'To stop the cars',
Or 'To start the next revolution'.

Then it grew into a beautiful flower,
Higher than all the tallest towers
And on its petals were solutions.

On some it said 'Breathe fresh air',
And on others 'Go back to mules',
Then passed over a cloud of fumes.

And the plant withered and died,
Then it said 'Look what pollution has done',
Then I realised, it was all down to me to stop pollution.

Georgia Marshall (11)
Lytchett Minster School

My Dream

I want to end world poverty,
I want a world that's happy too,
No arguments, no money that's owed,
I'd really like this to happen to the world.
I want the Earth to be a peaceful place,
Some place where you can unwind.
No turning on the TV and seeing atrocity,
It makes you feel sad for those who have to cope with it.
This is why I want the world to be a happier place.

Lucy Benjafield (11)
Lytchett Minster School

I Have A Dream

My brother is big, but not tall,
When I'm down he makes me feel big, not small.
My brother fought at war,
He makes my heart burn like the world's core.

Sometimes he shouts and likes to roar,
But at the end of it, he's as harmless as a boar.
He'll fix anything with his eyes closed,
He'll take you down with his bare toes.

He's big like a lion
And as strong as a block of iron.
He'll eat you like a piece of toast,
And could eat over a dozen roasts.

He can build something in five minutes,
If he were a doctor there would be so many cuts.
His hair is not short, but fairly long,
His muscles are the size of King Kong's.

My brother's daughter is like a cat,
Can crawl around as stealthy as a rat.
He shouts louder than my mum,
Probably because he has drunk too much rum!

William Gilligan (14)
Lytchett Minster School

Poem About My Grandad

The person I admire is my grandad.
I think he is great.
I like him more than my dad,
My grandad is my mate.
When I am sad, he is always there,
Sitting in his old-fashioned chair,
Sleeping everywhere.
This is my grandad,
He is the best,
Even when I am a pest!

Ross Chirnside (13)
Lytchett Minster School

Bill Bailey

I admire Bill Bailey, a funny guy,
A comic hero been through it all,
Like Moses to the Jews,
He fights for the children on the news.

His musical talent stands out strong,
The guitar and the keyboard, just like myself,
In the midst of the great Live Aid,
He rises to power, ruling is his fate.

His hair like sunshine, but a face like Hell!
His fingers stuck in the position of peace,
His message of racial harmony, strong as a rock,
The way that he rocks puts fighting to a stop.

He takes a leaf out of the killer whale's book,
The badger's face and the skunk's tail,
In the hope that the pandas turn out fine,
He puts two colours together like on the zebra's spine.

A hero like Superman, I bet he could fly!
He tells all the poor people not to cry.
He's the sun of the world,
The light of the moon,
Shame that he looks like a complete goon!

Liam Mullany (13)
Lytchett Minster School

Bob Geldof

I admire Bob Geldof.
I admire him because he helps people,
He cares for others,
Raising huge sums of money
And just gives it away.

I admire him because he raises awareness,
He does not act as a celebrity,
But uses his fame for good.

I admire him because he has it all,
He can have anything he wants,
Yet he still helps.

He buys his clothes from charity,
His food he grows organically,
He protests against the Third World debt,
He puts his pleas all over the Internet
And he won't just lose,
He'll keep fighting till he wins,
Not shove the protest in the bin.

And that's why I admire him,
He fights until he wins.

Alex Lovell (14)
Lytchett Minster School

You Never Know What You've Got Till It's Gone

My dad is the bravest person I know,
When he was only seven he had a major ear operation,
He was sick through worry,
But stayed strong and pulled through it.
In his teens he lost his dad,
And that set him right back to square one,
Just the safety of having a male around you,
He met my mum and soon after got married,
The best news came when they found out they would have a baby,
Nine months later she was on her way,
But the first sight of their baby was her foot,
So they were both rushed into theatre for an emergency operation.
He could have lost both of them,
Imagine that - your wife and child dying
And not even having a look at his new baby,
Or getting the chance to kiss his wife goodbye.
Then, after two more children
And another ear operation,
He split up with my mum.
His life came to a grinding halt and his world fell apart.
You never know what you've got till it's gone,
That's why I admire my dad.

Helen Ellis (14)
Lytchett Minster School

Imagination

The young girl sat, hunched in a dark corner,
Her body shivered and tears poured down like rain.
Everything she knew and loved had been taken from her,
However, one thing did remain.
This was her Heaven away from Hell,
Her sanctuary of peace and sunlight beams,
Her power of imagination and dreams.
So she shut her eyes tight,
Her body was still,
The weeping, taunting and horrible cries melted away,
Replaced by smiles, laughter and play.
No judging eyes,
No bloody fists,
No stabbing lies,
Just truthful bliss.
She imagines golden fields in the day,
Her sisters' smiling faces ask her to play.
The world is peaceful,
The world is well,
There is only Heaven here,
No nightmarish Hell.
Her eyes opened once more,
The dream world died.
Darkness she saw,
No matter how hard she tried.

Antonia Hollis (14)
Sherborne School for Girls

Imagine

Imagine a room full of people,
Imagine a crowd full of noise,
Imagine a world full of ignorance,
Imagine a silent voice.

Imagine a time where no one listened,
Imagine a time you turned a blind eye,
Imagine a time with no one caring,
Imagine the voice, still a cry.

Imagine always living alone,
Imagine crying each day,
Imagine never having a hope,
Imagine helped in no way.

Imagine being weak and desperate,
Imagine a big effort each day,
Imagine being invisible and alone,
Imagine just fading away.

Helena Maitland-Robinson (13)
Sherborne School for Girls

Imagine

I magine when global warming increases
M illions of playful children with gleeful faces
A ggressive tyrants wrapping their cages
G rieving families waiting . . .
I ce caps melting, nearby cities flooding
N ow despair covering everyone's emotions
E verything is dead, nothing left . . .

Louise Crowley (14)
Sherborne School for Girls

I Have A Dream

I have a dream,
That one day I will escape,
From these dreadful horrors surrounding me,
That one day I will find my destination,
But that is just a dream.

I have a dream,
That I may meet new people,
Even have friends,
Sometimes brought to laughter
And sometimes brought to tears,
But that is just a dream.

I have a dream,
That these dreams might go away,
My last shred of hope torn from my heart,
My body is empty, worthless,
In my mind I am terrified and sick,
But that is just a nightmare.

Pippa Jenkins (13)
Sherborne School for Girls

I Have A Dream . . .

I magine a place with no war,
M orning sun, peaceful land,
A gain and again happy faces,
G entle love spreading around,
I have a dream of continuous love and peace,
N o sadness in a world of peace,
E nd the wars around the world and my dream will come true.

But all this is a dream,
Dreams are fantasies,
They may be real,
Or they may be a flicker of hope in our mind,
I have a dream that this dream will happen.

Alice Hayes (13)
Sherborne School for Girls

I Have A Dream

I have a dream inside my head
That the world is at peace with one another.
That everyone loves their enemies like a brother,
One walks onto the street
And sees Americans and Iraqis meet.

I have a dream inside my head
That no one will argue or fight,
That everything will turn out right,
Now that it is the end of Apartheid,
Black and white can live without hate.

I have a dream inside my head
That there is no such thing as war,
That we can live in peace once more,
That there are no more bombs to kill
The innocent children. That's my will.

I have a dream inside my head
And while I'm kneeling by my bed,
I will wish and I will pray,
Who knows what will happen one day.

Tatiana Elwes (14)
Sherborne School for Girls

I Have A Dream!

I have a dream
An imaginary place
Where dolls come alive
And start a new race
Where all join as one
And learn to love!

Emma Welsh (14)
Sherborne School for Girls

Little Bluebird

Little bluebird soars in blue skies,
Wings flecked with golden sunlight.
High overhead he looks down and sings to the river,
The beautiful sorrow of the world.

He sees everything; sees blazing deserts,
Children's skeletons melting under the fiery sun.
Humans twisted obscurely by jealousy,
Faces scarred by dead memories and loss.

Young children's innocence stolen,
Along with all hope and love.
Plains cracked and dry like open mouths,
Begging silently for rain to drink.

People who've lost their footing in life,
Dreams that have been shredded or stained.
Cancer creeping up silently to linger,
Waiting for the right time to pounce.

Wings flutter with a rhythmic beat,
Aching with longing to change cruel into good.
Not to deliver perfection or close,
But to give the Earth its smile back.

Straining to flutter so hard,
Just for a smile.
Let my heart flutter with you little bird,
And sing to the river of peace.

Georgia Horrocks (14)
Sherborne School for Girls

I Want To Change The World

I want to change the world;
Make someone smile,
Make someone laugh,
End all wars,
End all quarrels,
Get everyone off the streets,
Get crime to stop;
I want to change the world.

I want to make a difference;
As much as I can make,
I want to stop the crying,
I want to stop the screaming.
It can't take much to give
Everyone smiles and laughter,
For just one day;
I want to make a difference.

I want to change the world;
I want love to conquer,
As knights do over dragons,
I want evil to go.
Can't everyone be thankful?
Can't people stop the wars?
I wish we had acted differently then;
I want to change the world.

Emily Rainbow (13)
Sherborne School for Girls

Imagine

Imagine my Heaven,
I am on top of the world,
The voice in the crowd,
The known name,
The light in the darkness who
Can make a difference.

Not for the moment though,
Not now, I am crushed by my family,
Teased by my age group,
Ignored by most,
Sometimes I wish I could sink into the ground,
Crawl around like an ant,
Small and inconspicuous.

Maybe one day,
My dreams may come true . . .
For now I have nothing,
Nothing but sleep,
But at least that's always there,
One thing in life to look forward to.

Alice Maltby (14)
Sherborne School for Girls

I Have A Dream

D reams are the only real things that live,
R ed is the blood that washes in the pain,
E very country is dead to all living things,
A reas of love are the only countries in the world,
M adness is the only form of sanity,
S mallest life is the largest hope.

Zoe Lodge (13)
Sherborne School for Girls

Imagine

Imagine no war,
Think of a place.
Imagine no poor,
Imagine a face.

Did you imagine somewhere precise?
Did you think of someone rich?
Did you imagine paradise?
Not somewhere in a ditch.

You can be poor, you can be strange,
Don't give up and leave.
Anyone can make a change,
Just go out there, believe.

Georgina Bolton Carter (13)
Sherborne School for Girls

Priorities

From the frosty streets of Harlem
To the agonising heat of Congo.
A baby howls,
A mother weeps,
For the hungry mouth she cannot feed.

And here I sit, fretting,
About the boy next door,
Or exams I may not pass.
When each day, worldwide,
There are many people struggling
Just to stay alive.

Jade Rickman (15)
The Grange School

A Perfect World Shopping List

No to homework
No to teachers
No to school
No to arguments
No to politicians
No to racists
No to poverty
No to injections

Yes to learning
Yes to best friends
Yes to home
Yes to making up
Yes to counsellors
Yes to friendship
Yes to equality
Yes to good health

No to nagging parents
No to bad TV
No to VCRs
No to sprouts
No to bullying
No to crime
No to rain
No to cold

Yes to happy mates
Yes to comedy
Yes to DVDs
Yes to chocolate
Yes to respect
Yes to relaxation
Yes to snow
Yes to warmth.

Oliver Frampton (15)
The Grange School

My Perfect World

In my perfect world, there would be no more world wars.
I would get rid of all the violence and I would get rid of all the laws.

I would fill the world with music and sounds
And I would give everyone a million pounds.

I would build my own skatepark, I would have lots of fast cars,
I would go to the shops and buy a million chocolate bars.

But the best thing about this place
Is that everyone has got a smile on their face.

Nick Gallop (15)
The Grange School

Survival?

Another night.
Such darkness.
Alone.
Wandering here, wondering why?
Peering through, observing life.
Though from the other side,
Of the window.
Rough, cold, dangerous,
Numb.
I see people, every day.
But they do not see me.
Scrounger, beggar, tramp,
Needy!
Nobody, to look out for me,
My necessities are few.
No job, no comfort, no family.
Still awaiting.
Abandoned.
Alone.

One way out.

Chelsie Andrews (16)
The Grange School

Shopping List For My Perfect World

No homework
No school
No skaters
No terrorists
No rats
No mice
No war
No boring TV
No racists
No poverty.

Adam Burtenshaw (14)
The Grange School

My Perfect World

In my perfect world there would be,
No war, just peace eternally.
Never knowing crime or harm,
Always feeling safe and warm.
No disasters ever happening,
Good health and peace for everyone.
The sun will shine, the rain will fall,
There will be food to feed us all.
No argument over religions and faiths,
One love will keep us all safe.
Rape and murder wouldn't exist,
Everyone would be happy and rich.
All your happiest dreams will come true,
In this perfect world for me and you.
No need for guns, bombs or knives,
No war to spoil or ruin lives.
Peace and joy and harmony,
Respect for whatever you may be.
No need for alcohol or drugs,
That poison people into thugs.
This is how my perfect world would be,
A perfect place for you and me.

Rosy Conner (15)
The Grange School

The Power Of One

I can change the world today and make a better place,
I will stop the violence for all the human race.
Riches I will give to the poor, if that is what they need,
As well as food and shelter, so they stay nice and clean.

Kindness costs nothing, you can give it away for free,
Just to stop and think awhile, for you, for them, for me.
I can change the world today and make a better place,
I can start the healing, in this time and in this place.

Daniel Sparkes (14)
The Grange School

My Perfect World!

My perfect world would have no room for war,
There would be plenty of food to go around,
And everyone can afford it because no one is poor,
If something is lost, you can guarantee it will be found.

There would be peace and harmony worldwide,
I suppose I'm like Martin Luther King because, I have a dream,
But John Lennon said, 'Imagine', so I tried,
And I came up with a plan for a world that won't fall apart at the seams.

Everyone would be different because that's what makes us,
No one will have to worry about insurgents because we're at peace
And you'll never have trouble trying to catch a bus,
Our world used to be like mine, but we couldn't afford the lease.

So as far as I can see,
This is how the perfect world should be.

Jonathan Bakes (15)
The Grange School

A Perfect World

My perfect world would be:
Not to have everyone suffering in the world,
Especially the children in poor countries,
Who don't have any food,
And in some parts of the world
They are losing their parents to AIDS
The world is a very sad place,
Especially in Great Britain.
There are so many children being killed,
We need to stop this now.
Get all the thugs out of here.
We want peace.

Rebecca Seymour (14)
The Grange School

Imagine

Imagine a world where no one was poor
Imagine a world where there was no war
Imagine a world where there was no hunger or strife
Imagine a world where there's no killing with knives.

Imagine a world where everyone was kind
Imagine a world where no one was deaf or blind
Imagine a world where everyone had money
Imagine a world where it was always sunny.

Imagine a world where it would never end
Imagine a world where everyone had a special friend.

Adam Dean (14)
The Grange School

The Stranger

A stranger can have a million personalities,
Depending on how you perceive them,
As a life of a mysterious man begins in my head,
I see aimless people, places and thoughts

I sit at a table, looking across at him,
The dark look of immorality stares back at me,
Never-ending this dream seems to be,
As absent-minded ideas frenzy erratically

I awake boldly, unaware of where I am,
Will I meet him again? Do I know him?
The stranger in my dreams is a mirror within me,
A flicker of my imagination.

Andrew Grantham (15)
Uplands School

Red Wood

I have a dream,
A dream which is a nightmare,
Dreamer,
Nothing but a dreamer,
They say.

Silly, stupid,
Pathetic they say,
You're just one person,
You can't change the world.

I can,
Why not,
Who says?
I can try.

I slice through
With the sleeping sword
Letting the poison bleed,
Ripping seam by seam,

Until the creeping moss
Lets the mighty
Redwood
Grow free.

I lie here
In the lush green meadows of peace,
While a thousand new souls
Are born into the
World

The deed is done.

Nabil Mahmoud (15)
Uplands School

Everyone Has A Dream

Walking onto the stage,
The crowd begins to cheer,
I pick up the mic,
Adrenaline takes over.

The costumes are ready,
Everyone is rushing,
The director shouts,
'Lights! Camera! Action!'

In my position,
Shotgun fires,
Streamlining the air,
Break the red ribbon.

Patient storms through the doors,
Ready to save a life,
Stand clear. Shocking.
His eyes open.

Alexandra Guerra Unwin (16)
Uplands School

I Have A Dream

An ambition
To go back in time, and change the past
The things I've done wrong
Regrets
I want to have good memories
Ones worth having
Ones worth telling
To change what I have done in certain situations
To be brave, not timid
Stand up for yourself
A different person.

Chloe Everett (15)
Uplands School

I Have A Dream

Vivid thoughts running freely through my mind
Like children in a playground.

People mixed up
In a maze of confused emotions.

Images painted untidily
With a brush of memories.

Past, present and future colliding into each other
Creating a whirlwind of thoughts.

My mind typing stories
That don't fit together.

Is it a twisted picture of the truth?

The wonder of realism or fantasy
As I wake up with palms of sweat.

Then not wanting to wake up
Closing my eyes tightly
Desperately seeking a conclusion.

And the sudden wave of happiness brought over me
As a fantasy is brought to life

My dream . . .

Rhiannon Wilson (16)
Uplands School

The Always Ending Story

Flying, swimming, walking, running,
I can go everywhere, anywhere I want,
In my mind I see forests, skies, rivers, seas,
I'm having fun, I know it's not going to last,
Then I wake . . . it always ends at the wrong time!

Phoebe Bowman (15)
Uplands School

Freedom Is A Virtue

Neutrality, integrity, virtue
Imagine an exemplary world
Most men's unblemished fantasies
Individual souls long for a moment
A moment like this, perfect!
A defiant stand towards justice
Lingering cries, still can be heard,
From past protests.
The cries of brave young men and women
Shadowing your every step.
They fought for a cause, one cause
To make freedom universal!
To make speech, liberate!
The power to be free and placid.

David Evans (14)
Uplands School

What Could It Be?

They are present in everybody's lives,
Some terrifying,
Some causing conundrum,
Taking you to regions where humans slave for animals,
Where water is supplemented by blood.

When they occur in the day,
They can be very dangerous,
Unexpected events take place,
People totally oblivious to their actions.

They make some people know,
Some people see,
Realising unwanted truths,
Everyone wakes in the morning to find it was vanity.

Chris Birtles (14)
Uplands School

Mourning And Night

Last night I awoke weeping.
Was that an illusion, or some kind of incubus?
A fantasy! Yes, of course!
It must be, for you were at my side.

Last night I missed you oppressively -
Have I told you?
When is your return?
I yearn to caress you.
Claim me with an amorous kiss.

Last night I had a cheerful nightmare!
I awoke breathless, like a fish out of water.
But now I'm over you! And you're at the bottom . . . of my heart.
I cannot resist.
We have an affair.
I persist.
I sleep and revere.
I think of you mourning and night . . .

Laura Edwards (15)
Uplands School

Poem

Sometimes, not often, I fantasize, I imagine,
Open up and wonder . . .
I begin to think of mythical beasts
Jetting white-hot shots of flame out of their flaming, blue nostrils.
A unicorn floats close by, twisting, turning,
Falling and rising, never faltering.
It lands and tosses its hair,
Making it wave like the silky waters of the seven seas.
I imagine also beautiful spectacles,
Like the sun setting into the green, lustrous fields of the Isle of Wight,
Dipping below the horizon, fading away behind the white,
                                        candyfloss clouds.
See you soon, I think to myself.

Daniel Bath (13)
Uplands School

What I Run From?

I'm running away
From these evil things
Which are truly strange

Some of these creatures
Have lots of scales
Or are very big, with giant teeth

A few will blend in
Some definitely not
But some just can't hide very well

Lots of them will tear you apart
But some won't even care
And a few will kill you for fun

As all these things chase me
I am so terrified
As I am scared of them eating me

But after all, I know this isn't real
And I know they won't do anything
So I am not really scared.

Oliver Shrimpton (14)
Uplands School

Fantasy Football

Weaving my magic, the crowd is impressed,
Deceiving defenders, I float past the tackles,
Finally in sight, the goal is waiting,
I pull back the trigger, only the goalie between us,
Unleashed like a comet, the ball heads for its target,
The goalie leaps skyward like a cobra awoken,
The goalie's effort is met with a roar,
But for right now, one-nil is the score.

Oliver Ricketts (11)
Uplands School

I Have A Dream

I have a dream,
My dream is for you,
Hating the role that you play,
Wishing you could have started
In life some other way.

You wished for changes as you went,
Chances to correct mistakes that you never meant,
And when you reached the final door,
You realised you couldn't wish anymore.

You may not have fulfilled all you wanted,
Others would say your life was stunted,
However, I always saw what may have been,
And I realised all that I had seen,

Was me,
Living that dream,
The dream I have,
Dreamt for you.

Ellen Walsh (16)
Uplands School

Olympic Sailing

I have an ambition in life which is,
To go to the 2012 Olympics,
To be a respected sailor in Britain,
Then to sail the speedy and the excellent Tornado,
To cross the line first,
To put the destination on my neck, the illuminated gold medal,
And win in a town that I used to sail in - Weymouth,
Also to stand on the podium cheering on the towering stand,
To be the youngest human to win a gold medal
And then to start all over again in the 2016 Olympics.

Christopher Tiernan (12)
Uplands School

My Life

I have many achievements I want to accomplish,
And many goals I hope to attain.
My life has many targets evolving around it,
Waiting out there, somewhere, to be found.
In my brief life I wish . . .
I become the most famous person,
Everyone would know me.
I become the richest person ever,
I could have whatever I desired.
I travel the whole wide world
And see all its famous wonders.
I live longer than anyone else,
So I'm never afraid of death.
I am the best at everything,
Then no one else can defeat me.
I'm not a greedy person, honestly!
Really, I'm as good as gold.
What I actually need to accomplish is to be happy and considerate,
Even if it means none of the above happening.
Because that is what definitely matters in life,
Despite what anyone else says!

Peter Dixon (16)
Uplands School

My Goal

To achieve my goal I must be fast,
Being fast isn't the only thing I need,
I need good reflexes and also a lot of stamina.

Now I can impress everyone with my skill,
I want to be able to play for my country,
From all this, I shall be known by many people.

To achieve my goal may take a long time,
It will also take a lot of effort,
But it will be worth it.

Otis Ooi (12)
Uplands School

The Images In My Head

The imagery in my head tells me wondrous stories and desires,
What I aim to do in the future, what I've done in the past,
Even what I do in the present all in one place,
A vibrant, colourful and imaginative mind of my own.

My wish for the future is to rule the golf course as a player,
The champion of skill and determination over many others,
But I would be a fair player towards others in the PGA Tour,
I would be a good sportsman, even if the game was not going well.

Another desire is to be able to take to the air with my own wings,
To soar above the clouds and down to the ground,
I would like to be able to simply travel anywhere I wanted,
To be done at the switch of a button and easily utilised.

The image I aspire to most is that I own a beautiful garden,
A sparkling utopia, full of nourishment and life,
A rich world to play or rest inside,
It would be just like my thoughts,
Locked up in myself,
My very own property.

Toby Adams (13)
Uplands School

My Poem

I want to entertain,
I want to be recognised,
To inspire
And to be successful.

I want to turn on the camera
And make blockbusters,
Action, horror, martial arts,
Whichever one
And last but not least,
I want to be remembered
As someone who entertains.

William Evans (12)
Uplands School

Fantasising

I sit in class all day, fantasising about boats
Splishing and splashing through the water
Gliding over the waves
Leaping out of the water, like a bullet leaving a gun
Speeding up the motor
Making it roar like a lion
The sun starts to set
I head back to the marina
Where the boat sleeps and rests
Wash it down and say goodbye
I then wake up and my delusion stops
The teacher shouts, I answer the question
And have my fantasy all over again.

Tim Johnson (13)
Uplands School

I Have A Dream

There can be no limitation to an ambition.
Desires are endless
Aims can be fulfilled with determination
Goals can be achieved without apprehension

Where poverty is extinguished
The homeless are shielded
World battles are abandoned

It would be a miracle for it to be reality
A flourishing atmosphere that fills the air.

Jennie Bird (16)
Uplands School

Find Another Day

A fantasy I long to fulfil is so distant.
Every morning I rise from my dull throne,
Walk down the tatty stairs,
Unconsciously, it seems.

Standing in my lonely kitchen,
I rub my furious eyes,
Preparing them for their responsible day.

My ambition pinches me!
The thought of being propelled into an ocean of stars
And falling endlessly into a stream of dark light,
Its mystical and enchanting nature,
Possesses a unique feeling inside of me.

Still unaided in my needy kitchen,
I feel insignificant,
Every day's repetitive events
Grow primitive in my disciplined mind.
I will tear through the stubborn womb of this Earth.
I will!

My vision is to one day shatter the seal,
Find another day.

Charlie Power (15)
Uplands School

Out Of Control

Uncontrollable thoughts engulf my mind,
Feeling powerless and feeble,
Some relaxing, some alarming,
Being submissive fills me with fear.

I occasionally awake with no sense of situation,
Oblivious and out of control,
Nothing around me seems familiar or recognisable,
My body is overpowered and I am vulnerable to attack.

Matthew Nisbet (14)
Uplands School

My Desire

I would be a world famous skater
And I would hang out with Bam Margera.
By 15 I would have a contract with 'Yeh Rite' Skate Company.
I would buy a massive mansion with a skatepark in it.
By 17 I would travel the world on a tour with Bam and some mates.
There would be thousands of skateboards.

I would sign autographs
And skate for charity for Third World countries.
I would buy them all skateboards.
I would slowly retire from skating.
I would find a good skater
And I would make them famous,
So they could live a good life.

Brandon Andrews-Hewitt (13)
Uplands School

The Dream Poem

My aim in life, I will be honest,
Is not for world peace or an end to hunger,
But to succeed.

I must admit that all people are too egotistical,
And I am sadly a full time member of this sick group.
The world has been consumed by greed,
No one cares for others, it's all me, me, me.

The Earth is being destroyed by us,
Our materialistic nature will destroy the human race,
Then, and only then will we finally be free.

Maybe now I have influenced your own dream.

Piers Bate (16)
Uplands School

When I'm Asleep

It soothes me to sleep,
It wakes me up in the early hours,
It puts fear into my mind,
It haunts me when I'm cheerful,
It haunts me when I'm depressed,
It never cheers me up,
I don't like this experience.

I strive to be a true hero,
I try to be the best,
I dream of being the finest,
I practise to achieve the highest level,
I cannot stop thinking of this dream,
It is my destiny,
I believe this dream will become reality.

Toby Hoare (15)
Uplands School

I Have A Dream

I have a dream
I dream of
Peace, not war
Food, not hunger
Water, not drought
Money, not poverty
Health, not illness
Truth, not lies
Happiness, not crime
Life, not death
That's my dream.

Helen Day (15)
Uplands School

Paradise

Wrapped like a warm blanket,
I lie in the sand,
Feeling the grains,
Running through my hands.

The gentle waves lapping,
Onto the perfect shore,
The distant voices,
Of happy swimmers.

A soft breeze,
Playing around me,
Like a gentle massage,
I never want to end.

Foreign voices and strange faces,
Everything so unfamiliar,
I am in paradise . . . I'm sure I was.

Toby Khalife (14)
Uplands School

I Want, I Wish, I Imagine!

I want to see,
I want to feel,
I want to taste,
I want to make a difference.

I wish I could be there,
I wish I could be noticed,
I wish I could help,
I wish I could meet new people.

I imagine new lands,
I imagine secretly inhabited islands,
I imagine hidden corners of the Earth
. . . or maybe another planet.

Jessica Bishop (11)
Uplands School

My Indonesia

It is thousands of miles away
I left you for my future
I've lived in Bournemouth now
For several years

I miss your warm weather
Your lovely thousand islands
Childhood friends
Nice smiling faces

Here
I make a lot of friends
I learn different cultures
And language

I remember what the Wise Man said,
'Learning is part of our life
No matter where it is
Try to love it'

There is good and bad everywhere
Take the good
Get rid of the bad
It will make my life better in the future

Now I know
The world is big
Different people
Different ways of life

I have to learn
Very hard
Try to understand it
For my benefit

Even though
I still miss you, Indonesia
Wait for me
Someday I will return to you.

Rachmat Akbar Triyadi (12)
Uplands School

I Wish . . .

I wish I could swim
Deep in the ocean
Swim through stormy seas
Glide through silky waters

I wish I could swim
In and out of oceans
Jump so high and dive
Back into the sea

I wish I could swim
So fast I can't see
Swim too deep
And hide in the darkness

I wish I could swim
So close to shore
So people could see me
And shout happily

I wish I could swim
So slowly and calm
Glide so smoothly
Until I die.

Sophia Bird (11)
Uplands School

Cool!

Smart clothing and gear,
Thinking it is cool.
Going up and up into the cold blowing on your face
Like millions of splinters pricking you,
Soon at the top, a trail of kids behind,
Then shooting down hills,
Impressed by the kids doing this fun event,
Blue, red and black, the three stages,
The kids taking it as if it were flat,
Thinking they're cool, until a big pile of kids,
Some crying, some laughing,
Still in one piece,
Trying to help, then quickly all of the kids
Up and off,
Amazed by the sight,
Laughing your eyes out,
As if someone is tickling you with a feather,
Checking your watch and looking at the map
To see what the easiest way back is,
Zipping from hill to hill,
Suddenly a group of nannies, mums and dads
Waiting for their son or daughter at the bottom,
Kids showing off,
Parents laughing,
Kids going to parents,
Going home to your chalet,
Having a hot chocolate,
Cake, TV and biscuits,
Watching sports and getting tips for the future,
In front of the warm fire, which is delightful,
Having a nap and dreaming of the exciting day you've had.

Jack Fuller (12)
Uplands School

Snow Dream

Dashing left and right, past rocks and trees
Speeding into the air, I complete a few tricks before landing
I have to keep my knees bent and I am covered in snow
Travelling at a very fast speed, whilst keeping my balance
I need to keep myself streamlined.

Riding with the wind
Jumping over a fallen tree, I execute a forward flip
I accelerate down a steep slope
Scattering pieces of buried tree everywhere
I can feel the cold slapping my face as the speed intensifies
But it doesn't bother me in the slightest.

My mind wanders back to the start of the race
And I almost lose my balance
Fortunately, I manage to turn quickly
At a very sharp corner, just in time
The professional skills I have acquired
Have stopped me from losing this race.

I am wearing a jacket, baggy trousers
And selected accessories for this sport
All of which are in my favourite colours
My body feels warm, even though the sun is setting.

I know that there is nobody in pursuit
In the distance I see a shimmering banner
Stretched between two poles
There is a large silhouette behind this
And I can only imagine that this must be the waiting crowd.

The race is now complete as I fly under the finishing line
And the crowd cheers deafeningly
I am the champion now
Waiting for that large, glistening cup.

Thomas Beesley (11)
Uplands School

The Seasons

Children at the beach playing in the sand,
While the elderly sit and watch time go by.
Farmers in the orchard picking fruit from the tree,
While their wives are inside, making fruit jam.

Soon the leaves will fall,
And the apples go all mouldy,
The beach is deserted, no one in sight,
Whilst the last blooms fade.

Children out in the snow,
While families sit around the fire,
Eating mince pies,
As robins try to find crumbs in the snow.

The daffodils start to bloom,
While the smell of newly cut grass is in the air.
The apples are starting to grow,
While the children play in the garden.

I wish it was always like this.

Joshua Boer (10)
Uplands School

Difference

I would like to be seen, noticed, heard,
Make a difference, be able to shout out loud
And everyone hears me.
Feel your heart racing
Like a car going round in a circle,
Then suddenly it slowly gets slower and slower
And you think it's all ended, but no . . .
Bang!
Your soul feels like it's being shot at by guns,
But just missing you by one centimetre.
You see loads of faces staring at you
And when you blink, you think to yourself,
Wow! Have I, me, really made a difference?

Isabel Breslin (11)
Uplands School

The Winning Post

I wish I could jump up into the sky and make it go faster
So I can reach somewhere nice to eat and drink
When we get there the breeze will stop and we'll slow down
Off we go, galloping again
It twinkles in the blue, shining sea
It's near the end of the race, I was in my dream
My heart was thumping
I turned around and people were behind me
I was first, there was the finish line
I was there, I won
I was the champion
I jumped up in the air and shouted, 'Yeah!'

Megan Creed (10)
Uplands School

Silver Seas!

I wish I could feel the sand beneath my feet,
The sun on my back,
The wind in my face.

Like a dolphin gliding through silver seas,
Like a shark never turning back,
Keeping focused on that one tunnel ahead,
Not the road behind.

I want to feel like a caterpillar,
Emerging from its chrysalis,
That feeling I'd feel,
The feeling of freedom.

Georgie Rowbrey (11)
Uplands School

Runner

I was tossing and turning
I couldn't get to sleep
Then at half-past twelve, finally I did

I was waiting, nervous, eager
And excited at the same time
Hardly able to eat
Half-past two, five minutes to go!
One minute and here we go!
The whistle was blown
Down the track I raced

I could hear the crowd roaring
And the sun on my face
I daren't look behind me.

The blood was pumping through my veins
Adrenaline was too!
I just had to keep telling myself to carry on.

The end was getting closer
There was nobody in front of me
And there it was, the finish line!
I slammed through the tape
Exhausted and red in the face.

The announcement was made
I was triumphant
The gold was mine
Panting and puffing
I slurped down water
Tears in my eyes
I was so excited
With everyone cheering and applauding my name
I had done it!

Megan Hallowes (10)
Uplands School

I Have A Dream - What A Hit!

What is happening? I cannot see,
I am being engulfed by something,
But, what is it?
Then, quite suddenly, it comes back to me,
The sights, and the touch,
Of the object that will make me famous,
Well, one day.

The sweaty feel of the clothes
I am wearing,
The soft feel of the wood.
Suddenly, the orb is flying,
All rounded and shiny,
With the crowd in the background
Calling my name.
They are making me famous,
Well, until another day.

Then, without warning, the item was airborne again,
Flying, flying, flying, far away,
And then, the heap on top of me,
The stench of sweat reeking in my nose.
I am now famous,
Well, until another day.

Jacob Webster (10)
Uplands School

My Dream Love

I waited at the station for my love and beauty
It caught my attention that she was with another man
I went home
I mentioned it to my friends, it was a dark situation for me
I made a descriptive poem about my love and carried on
                                        without my rose.

I carried on into the winter
She walked past and didn't take any notice
I saw in her eyes she was loved forever and ever
For eternity.

Time raced on into spring
All the leaves growing
Making parks clean
With my girl at the tree, making up a melody.

Summer comes
All the leaves, beauty of the Earth
With all the roses
I grew them
And watched forever and ever
With all my love blown off in the winter.

Jack Notley (11)
Uplands School

My Ambition

If I had an ambition, it would be to become a famous actor
And meet all the famous stars, like George Clooney,
Brad Pitt, Harrison Ford, Ben Stiller and Owen Wilson.
I imagine that I could be in some of the big films,
To make enough money to buy extravagant gifts for my family.
One day I hope to buy a gigantic yacht to sail around the world
And meet all the different kinds of people.
Another one of my ambitions is to donate a lot of money to charity.
I think that doctors should earn more money than football players,
After all, they are saving people's lives.

Jonny Summerell (12)
Uplands School

What I Want To Be - My Dream

I'm running down the field
Wiping the sweat off my brow
With the ball in my possession
All the opposition on my tail
I was so close to the try line
But the opposition caught up
And took me down
I threw the ball to my teammate
As he ran down the field
He dives to the ground
The ref blows his whistle
Our team are under pressure
Try given
Our team cheering
The opposition are angry
The whistle blows
I charged towards the other team
I take down their best player
And I have the ball in my grasp
I dived for the ground
'Try given,' the ref said
The ref blows his whistle
End of match
The crowd cheering
We've won!

Zack Dalton-Biggs (11)
Uplands School

My Dream

It's time to go on, I'm mounted and ready,
I'm waiting and hoping, I'll get past,
It's 2012, I'm here, I know what it feels like.

I'm on, I'm here, I'm ready, there goes the beep,
I'm trotting, faster and faster, canter, jump 1, jump 2,
The more jumps I do the better I get,
One foul, don't look back, and now jump number 9,
I've finished,
It's 2012, I'm here, I know what it feels like.

Now the scores. I'm 4th,
No medal but I'm not walking home,
I'm battling on,
It's 2012, I'm here, I know what it feels like.

My horse is tired, we need a relaxing night's rest,
Tomorrow's the big day, am I trotting home?
Or cantering forward?
It's 2012, I'm here, I know what it feels like.

And now again, no foul,
I've done it, I'm first,
I'm galloping forward until I win again,
And again,
It's 2012, I'm here, I know what it feels like.

The crowds are like roaring lions,
They surge forward
And now my cup,
I've reached my gold,
I feel exhilarated,
It's 2012, I'm here, I know what it feels like.

Angharad Burn (11)
Uplands School

My Inspiration

I'm leaping gracefully,
Across the mats;
I perform a couple of front flips
And I land in the splits.
People are cheering,
Some calling my name;
I jump off the mats,
I'm excited and proud.

I'm steadying myself,
On the beam;
I stand on tiptoes,
So that I can fit on.
I pull into a cartwheel
And I land on my feet;
I'm having a fantastic time
And the crowd is cheering.

Jordana Coulstock (11)
Uplands School

When I'm Older - My Dream

To push myself down the lane
To make sure I get that medal
I'm aiming for gold
I must keep at it
I must not give up
I'm really worn out
I'm still going for it
The wall is getting closer
The other contestants are tailing behind me
Closing the gap
Wearing me out.

Robert Bell (11)
Uplands School

A Boy

The world on his shoulders,
Twelve years old, a genius,
A healer,
A god . . .

Another child,
He loves cricket
In the dusty streets he plays
Dancing with his cousins, his confidence shines through.

This is no ordinary Indian boy
Medical students from the world over, are mesmerized
                              by his knowledge
Intellectuals are amazed by his simple formulae.

He will cure cancer
He will cure AIDS
He wants to stop the suffering of every human, curing every disease.

We cannot let this star burn out,
He's up in the mountains, in India, just like a god,
Don't put the world on his shoulders, remember -
He is a boy.

Jack Kane (15)
Uplands School

Flying In The Sky

Flying through the air
At hundreds of miles per hour
Just me on my own
No one to bother me

Nearing the Earth
Soon to deploy my parachute
Coming towards my friends
Ready to land.

Lewis Tottle (13)
Uplands School

The Fanatical Assault

I was there in the back of the truck waiting for extraction,
Sliding off the vehicle, quickly surveying the area,
Giving the all-clear, I bungeed through metal fire to access cover.

So I pondered my surroundings with a water pistol in my
pillow-sized hands,
Accepting it as real life and shooting teddy bears at the skeletons,
Smashing them to smithereens, I led my men into enemy territory,
And before my eyes was the eye-blinding quilt covered flag.

Crouching under cotton rubble,
McDonald grabbed the flag vigorously,
Protecting his back with my suppressive fire, I followed,
The archway ahead was the way out of the pillow-feathered building.

Anthony Skilton (14)
Uplands School

Football - My Dream

I've gone out through the tunnel
Onto the pitch to come to a grinding halt
To see everyone there shouting my name
My heart pounding, I'm through on goal
To win the World Cup for my team
Suddenly, my legs have snapped like a cocktail stick
At least I've won my team a penalty
But this could be the end of my career
I've been stretchered off
But my team smash the ball in the back of the net
That was satisfying.
That's my dream!

Sam Hardinges (11)
Uplands School

Breathe In

The almighty heavens caving in at once
Super novas flashing before my eyes
Shooting stars, some burning, some frozen
Overtaking me.

The concave universe imploding itself
Into a minute piece of dust
Now it's just me on my own
Floating in an endless place of nothing.

Pure white, pure clean . . . nothing
But then, in this haven of tranquillity
The microscopic speckle of dust floats before my eyes
And then . . .
Inhale, I take a gasp of air to fill my vacant lungs
And in flows the tiny speckle of dust
Of what the universe had become.

James Creevy (14)
Uplands School

My Goal

When I grow up I want to cross the finish line in 1st position
It's all about speed - how fast can I go?
I must stay upright - I cannot fall
I'm wearing a number - it's 10
Can I do it?
Any mistakes and I'll be disqualified

Faster and faster
Swishing and swinging in and out of the red flags
People cheering - they want me to win
How good will it feel to win the gold in the Winter Olympics?
I'm cold and wet, but I've won
I feel fantastic.

James Cull (10)
Uplands School

What's The Point?

What's the point?
You're so annoying,
I can't believe it,
You're still destroying.

What's the point?
You're so destructive,
In the real world,
You're more seductive.

What's the point?
There's so much violence,
Too many guns,
There is no silence.

The storm is rough,
The sea is wavy,
Why did I dream,
To join the Navy?

Oliver McMillan (11)
Wareham Middle School

My Dream

T he lights shining on my face
O utstanding team to help me look my best

B eth, my name in lights
E veryone focusing on me as I sing

A ll the lyrics to learn

S inging my heart out
I 'd never get bored
N ever-ending autographs
G oing to
E xotic places on tour
R ain or shine.

Bethany Ritchie (12)
Wareham Middle School

I Have A Dream

My trees sway, my mountains are still,
Strong, rocky, steep and tall,
The trees are asking questions,
My hills are answering,
Curing their puzzled faces.

Branches crackling under an invisible foot,
My neighbour is the air,
Passers-by never come,
I'm lonely,
In need of a friend.

I would love to hear
Singing voices,
Or feel footsteps on my earth,
Have children climbing
My beloved trees.

I have a great dream,
To bring people to my world,
Bring sun or rain,
I dream of change,
Good change.

I dream for lots of trees to grow,
For people to admire them,
For everyone to enjoy them,
For the sun to shine on them,
For the rain to shower them.

I wish all these things
Would come soon to me,
Wonderful things,
Change,
I have a dream.

Rachel Woolley (11)
Wareham Middle School

My Dreams

I have a dream that one day
The world will be a happier place
It will come true!

I have a dream that one day
Every different personality will live as one
It will come true!

I have a dream that one day
The world will be at peace with one another
It will come true!

I have a dream that one day
All animals will be treated fairly
It will come true!

I have a dream that one day
Bullying will stop
It will come true!

I have a dream that one day
Everyone will be classed as equals
It will come true!

I have a dream that one day
One of these dreams will become reality
That definitely will come true!

Holly Elliott (11)
Wareham Middle School

I Have A Dream

I have a dream that one day,
Chocolate will rule the world,
Because you could eat their armies!
I have a dream that one day,
Grown-ups will be children,
Because then you could tell them what to do!
I have a dream that one day,
I will be rich and famous,
Because then I could have a room for my shoes!
I have a dream that one day,
Bullies will be spotty,
Because then they would know what it feels like to be laughed at!
I have a dream that one day,
This poem will be recognised,
Because it will prove dreams can come true!

Hattie Stewart (12)
Wareham Middle School

I Have A Dream

I have a dream that I'm a cat
And sit around all day,
I pounce and prance and leap and sleep
And run around and play.

I have a dream that I'm a fish
And through the water glide,
I shoot and dart and somersault
And on the current, ride.

I have a dream that I'm a bird,
Soaring through the sky,
I dip and dive and flit about
And see things from up high.

Joseph Ely (11)
Wareham Middle School

I Have A Dream

I have a dream,
I'm by a stream,
Fairies are everywhere
And they're playing with my hair.

And underneath the sun's warm glow,
The willows and the bluebells grow,
Sir Lancelot comes riding by,
Under the bold and bright blue sky.

He picks a bluebell from a bunch
And hands it to me with my lunch,
We sit and chat on the bank side,
And then my eyes spring open wide.

And all of a sudden I wake up,
The dream has ended - just my luck!

Molly Irwin (12)
Wareham Middle School

I Have A Dream

I have a dream to fly away
And come back when the sky is blue
And the sun is bright.

To ride away
And come back when the grass is green
And the rivers are clean.

To swim away
And come back when the shore is clear
And the tide is high.

To walk away
From all my fears and troubles
And come back when the world is at peace.

Ella Ward (12)
Wareham Middle School

I Have A Dream

People ask you 'What's your dream?'
Some people say to be rich and mean
Some people say to be famous and wealthy
Others say to be very healthy.

But my dream's different from the rest,
I wish that everyone would have success
No wars or cancer will exist
And every person will get kissed.

Families will be brought together
In natural harmony forever
Babies will be born everywhere
And they will be treated with lots of care.

Some dreams can come true
But that's mostly for a lucky few
I hope that I am one of these
Then I will be very pleased!

Carly Hutchins (12)
Wareham Middle School

I Have A Dream

I have a dream to be a footballer
I have a dream to be able to do magic tricks
I have a dream to be a little smaller
I have a dream to go to the Olympics

I have a dream to play rugby
I have a dream of a free Tibet
I have a dream to end poverty
I have a dream of a world without regret

I have a dream to stop smoking
I have a dream to go to five paces
I have a dream to stop drug doping
I have a dream to do a police case.

Sam Duffield (11)
Wareham Middle School

When I Grow Up

When I get a job,
I wondered, sipping my beer,
I want to enjoy the job,
So I began to think of ideas.

I quite fancied being a tennis player,
But then I decided, not my thing,
What about a pop star?
But I can't even sing.

Being in a circus would be fun,
Gymnastics would be sporty,
I could be an assassin,
But that would be naughty.

I don't want to be a scientist,
I'd rather not be a gardener,
Although it would be quite fun
To be a racing car designer.

But I don't want to do any of those,
I've got my ideas all set.
There is only one job for me
And that's to be a vet!

Alex Rainbird (11)
Wareham Middle School

Dreaming

There once was a man who dreamed,
That nothing was quite as it seemed.
He thought the Earth was made of chocs,
And thought his shoes were his socks,
That silly old man who dreamed.

Martin Buxton (11)
Wareham Middle School

I Have A Dream

I have a dream
Of happy children,
Not hungry kids,
History is poverty,
Future is plenty.
Not living in prison for what you said,
Telling the truth out loud instead.
Not to walk in the fields full of dread,
But to walk on the green grass of plenty with every tread.
Not to hear bombs and cries
And see little children with tears in their eyes.
We leave it to our leaders and pray they'll be wise,
If a few people had a *lot* less -
A lot of people would have *enough*.
This is my dream.
    Stop it all now!

Eden Midgley (11)
Wareham Middle School

I Have A Dream

I have a dream,
That there will be world peace.

I have a dream,
That there will be no more poverty.

I have a dream,
That I will be a forensic scientist.

I have a dream,
That there will be no more racism.

I have a dream,
That I will be able to do magic tricks.

I have a dream,
That everyone will be safe and happy
And the world will never end.

Charles Fishlock (12)
Wareham Middle School

I Had A Dream

I had a dream
That the skies weren't blue.

I had a dream
That there was no me or you.

I had a dream
That there was no war.

I had a dream
That there were no laws.

I had a dream
That people were rich.

I had a dream
That the whole world could switch.

I had a dream
That no one would be poor.

I had a dream
Where there was a big door.

I had a dream
That I walked through the door
And guess what I saw?
It was reality.

Daizee-Laine Napier (11)
Wareham Middle School

I Have A Dream!

I have a dream,
That one day there will be no war.

I have a dream,
That one day there will be no poverty.

I have a dream,
That one day people won't be homeless.

I have a dream,
That one day there will be peace.

I have a dream,
That one day there will be no crime.

I have a dream,
That one day there will be no fighting.

I have a dream,
That one day there will be no more arguing.

I don't need a dream,
To realise that my dreams won't ever come true!

Marcia Gaskell (12)
Wareham Middle School

I Have A Dream

I have a dream,
That one day children will not be forced to do homework.
If they don't do it,
Sometimes they are treated like jerks.
To kids, homework is their worst nightmare.
To teachers, they find it funny when it gives the kids a scare.

If it were up to kids about homework,
They'd definitely say no more,
Then teachers would be bored, for sure.
The parents try to give the best encouragement to the kids,
Only to find that the kids just say,
'I wouldn't do it for a hundred quid!'

Children think that the work should be done at school,
Because they'd rather be outside playing with their brand new balls.
Teachers say school would be extended if there was no homework,
But sometimes, the teacher says it with a small smirk!

Cameron Slacke (12)
Wareham Middle School